SERVANT
LEADER MINDSET

Transforming your leadership style from the
inside out

SHANNON M. LEE

DEDICATION

This book is dedicated to every person who thinks they are stuck with the way they experience everyday work. There is a better way and it is yours for the taking.

CONTENTS

Acknowledgments

ACKNOWLEDGMENTS

Thank you to my husband Kristofer. Kris, you patiently waited on me to join you in Netflix binges, pizzas and conversation while I wrote and edited this book, all without one complaint. You knew how important this project was to me and cheered my efforts every step of the way. Thank you, so much-your support and enthusiasm, means the world to me.

To so many who inspired me along the way...

The Relā Board of Directors who responded with genuine enthusiasm when I told them of this book idea.

The innumerable Columbus, Ohio community members who have attended my workshops, read my blogs and emails; who vulnerably shared their workplace struggles with me and gave me feedback on my ideas. You continue to inspire me every day.

Finally, my dad, Jeff Buswell (RIP). You always said I could do whatever I wanted to do, I just needed to figure out what I wanted to do. Well, dad-I wanted to write a book so here it is!

INTRODUCTION

Servant leadership at its core is about caring for people, specifically in the workplace. Caring for people in the workplace requires active participation in the identification of other people's needs and wants; evaluating the impact of those needs and wants and then making decisions that are in the best interest of the greatest number of people. The servant leader cares enough to do this because the servant leader understands that people are a priority over profits. Furthermore, the servant leader believes that one does not have to choose between people and profits, because they have developed emotionally to the point where they can hold space for the "both-and".

In this, the prime motivator for a servant leader is to serve others by helping them develop as people, professionals and contributors to the community. For too long, the 'serve' in servant leadership was presumed as weakness and an inability or unwillingness to address tough situations or have hard conversations. The avoidance of such things prohibits the growth of people, so a true servant leader does not avoid the hard stuff at work. However, the servant leader approaches those tenuous situations in a way that puts people and their development first. The "how" matters. This unwavering commitment to a person-first

1

approach can be misconstrued, nonetheless.

To be clear, when I say 'serve' I do not mean the servant leader turns into a martyr, doing everything for others and sacrificing to the detriment of self. Sacrifice is involved in servant leadership, but not to the detriment of one's own needs or others. I cannot give what I do not possess, so as a servant leader, who I am, what I can do, what I know, how I feel, how I show up…matters.

A Note About Faith

Faith is a central part of my life; however, I do not believe faith of any kind is necessary to embrace servant leader ideas and mindsets. While there are those who may believe servant leadership has its roots in ancient religious traditions, the style of servant leadership need not be religious. You will see me make mention of faith in my life and story because it is part of my authentic self. Faith is a part of my journey both as a person and a leader. I cannot separate the two. I fully recognize my experience is not shared by all and while I may refer to my faith at times, I do not do so in an exclusionary way. The ideas and mindsets in this book are available to anyone interested regardless of where the reader stands on matters of faith.

MY FIRST BIG JOB

In 2001, I embarked on my first leadership experience. While I believe we are all leaders and I was leading myself up until this point, this was the first time I was responsible for others. My role as an elementary school principal at a private, religious school involved *all the things*. I hired, fired, wrote people up, developed performance plans, marketed and helped recruit for the school, wrote marketing copy, produced videos, attended school plays and concerts, ran awards ceremonies and chapels, ran staff meetings and in-service trainings, disciplined students, and counseled parents.

And I was twenty-eight years old.

From the daycare to sixth grade, I was responsible for thirty-some teachers, over three hundred and fifty kids, and developing positive relationships with parents, stepparents, grandparents, etc. I could not believe the number of people who wanted to meet with me on any given day. I made plans for my day and ninety percent of the time they were shot to hell because of student behavior issues, urgent parent meetings and various unforeseen circumstances. Looking back, almost every single day felt unforeseen. All my strategic tasks were pushed back yet again while I put out fires and wiped noses for six more hours. And, as a mother of young children myself, working in the evenings was required and became quite the juggling act between homework, dinner, and bedtime stories. This, of course, on the evenings I wasn't at the school until seven o'clock trying to get something on my task list done.

Most days I was mildly overwhelmed and on the other days I was utterly inconsolable with anxiety. I remember no easy days. I neither felt victory, nor could celebrate when a victory came. Every interaction was wrought with stress and immense self-doubt, not to mention the inevitable post-interaction hangover, where I questioned my every word, facial expression, and even intentions.

I distinctly remember escaping to the girls' bathroom (no staff bathroom in my wing) to just breathe and escape the pressure of my role, if even for five minutes.

I felt like I had no idea what I was doing. I was caught between wanting to lead and feeling completely unprepared for leadership. No one forced me to accept this position. My own desire to lead and unshakable belief that I could make a difference kept me in this job.

In all, I stayed in this position for five years and as those years progressed, I experienced the problems of the day with increasing pain and began to anticipate future problems by making them up in my head. You could say I became an expert in borrowing trouble from the future. I expected bad things to happen, mistakenly believing if I could imagine them first, they might not be so tough when they occurred. I didn't know it then, but this new habit of borrowing problems from the future completely changed how I showed up at work in the present moment.

I wanted to be one hundred percent sure I didn't let anyone down. Disappointing people, getting it wrong, and making a mistake: those things felt like death sentences to this young leader who wanted so desperately to prove, "I have what it takes."

I did all this in the name of servant leadership. Looking back, I probably equated this service, this sacrifice, with serving God too, which was oh, so very off the mark. And while I was influenced by wanting to make a difference, the pain was coming from the avoidance of failure. Looking back, I am confident of this one thing: the force driving me was not *caring for people*. The driving force was *pleasing people*.

Caring for people and pleasing people are two different motivators.

I had no idea how to best serve the people around me; I had no clue how to serve the vision I was a part of. I only knew how to take cues from those people and try to do what they wanted to keep them happy and approving.

Eventually I burned out and left. I believed my problem was related to the place and a new environment would bring the change I needed. Yes, a geographical relocation was just what I needed.

NEW HORIZONS

One of my favorite parts of being a principal was helping teachers create and work on personal/professional development plans. I figured, if I could get some experience in the corporate world doing this very thing, I'd have it made. I sought out roles in learning and development and corporate training. However, I quickly learned, ten years in private, Christian education didn't translate well into the corporate sector. In fact, they didn't even consider my five years as a principal "management experience". What a rude awakening! Eventually I found a job, just not the role I was after. It took about six months, but I got a job as an Executive Assistant in one of our community's largest employers. I heard good things about this company and really felt lucky to land the job even if it wasn't at all what I wanted to be doing for a living.

As I moved to the corporate world, I found a lot of differences but what didn't change was me. This was a stunning and sad realization. I still felt angst when completing projects. I still projected bad outcomes into the future, and then tried to prevent that through present-day manipulation tactics. I still struggled with work-related anxiety, despite the fact that my new corporate job had very clear boundaries and, comparatively, greatly reduced stress. And nobody cared if I went above and beyond. They only cared if I stayed in my lane.

Why was this a problem? Going above and beyond was how I received validation. In my job at the school, doing more, more, more was the goal. Now my new boss just wanted me to do my job description. What?

Don't get me wrong. The expectations in that job description were high and there was zero flexibility for a lack of performance (that part I loved). But I learned quickly to not ask to do something that wasn't my job. Innovation and pushing to change old paradigms were not needed from me.

The company I worked for, while known for its positive culture, had a very subtle but distinct boys' club, still common in more places than some like to admit. As a woman, I can only say how it made me feel. There were few women in leadership, and the ones who were in leadership were bad-mouthed by some of the men behind the scenes You hear a lot as an assistant, and I heard it regularly. The message that was communicated, even if unintended, was this: women aren't seen as viable leadership. While my intention is not to bash any former employer, as this particular one gave me many valuable leadership lessons, this experience caused me to realize something startling about myself.

The revelation that no one needed or wanted me to

achieve was damaging to my identity. My identity was rooted in what I could accomplish; specifically, what I could accomplish beyond what my boss has asked me to do. How could I ever really feel fulfilled here? How could I advance so that I could further prove myself?

Today, I realize at least some of my perceptions about the opportunities there were skewed by these identity issues. I was just unaware.

I actually stayed there for seven years. All in all, that place was a good place to work, great benefits, and I made some very good friends. And when I left that role, I wasn't looking for a job. A job came knocking, the job I am in now.

BACK TO NONPROFIT

Running a nonprofit has given me two huge gifts: First, the chance to run an organization, something I've always wanted. Second, professional challenges that have forced me to change what caused all the pain I previously described. I'll admit, my misguided need to achieve and perform is what drove me to my current role. I was so motivated by the opportunity! This is further proof to me that my problem wasn't the job but rather my mindset. Still, it is here in this role where I learned many of the new mindsets I share in this book.

I began my new job as an Associate Director and I really thought all my dreams had come true. Translation: all my professional pain would end. When I found I once again experienced the same pain as my previous roles, I figured it out. I've never been good at math, but I realized, *I was the common denominator*.

I really thought I was a servant leader by nature, but I actually knew very little about the leadership style until I began my current role. And, as an organization whose platform is servant leadership, it was a good idea for me to learn.

So, I did.

What I have uncovered over the last five years or so

has quite literally transformed my life; and not just my professional life. What I have learned about servant leadership has spilled over into my personal life and there isn't one single relationship that does not benefit from this new way of showing up.

Servant leadership is a leadership style, yes. Servant leadership is a way of *doing* leadership, most definitely. But doing servant leadership and becoming a servant leader are two very different things. Showing people how to do something is an important step, but the most exciting experience in personal and professional development is when people *embody that which they desire to become*. For example, when someone fundamentally changes how they think about the treatment of others, they no longer have to be told how to treat people with care and concern. The care and concern flow quite effortlessly.

What I learned about changing how I experienced the world and specifically, my leadership role, is what this book is about. This is not a book about the steps to *doing* servant leadership. This is a book about *becoming* a servant leader. By developing a servant leader mindset, I believe the actions of servant leadership are more and more a natural and fundamental part of how one shows up.

I am not an academic or a researcher, although much of what I've learned and applied comes from those types of people. I offer to you simple (but not easy) and impactful approaches to begin to embrace and embody a new way of showing up at work and in life that will enable you to actually serve those around you *without losing you*. In fact, you'll find *more of you* on this journey.

As you move forward in this book, my hope for you is to develop the mindset that creates a more natural set of strategies and skills which result in the type of person anyone would want to follow, even if you have no clout, no official title, or fame.

1
FOUNDATION: A MODEL FOR SERVANT LEADERSHIP

Understanding leadership styles was never important to me. This admission may sound strange coming from someone writing a book on servant leadership, but it's true.

Like many I've met along the way, I stumbled into servant leadership largely due to pain. In 1995, I entered a fifth-grade classroom, fresh out of college. If I'm honest, my entire motivation for choosing education was two-fold: no tough math classes in college and summers off. Seriously. Coursework and vacation time were the two driving forces pushing me into the elementary classroom.

You're impressed, I know.

Nonetheless, I cared deeply about performing well in general, and spent hours on lesson plans, carefully graded papers, and did my very best to have thoughtful conversations with anxious parents. And while many days it seemed nothing I did made any difference in the lives of those kids, I developed a general affinity for the teaching process and experienced some good outcomes. I was serving.

Or so I thought.

8

To me, servant leadership was about doing, doing, doing for others. I made it my goal to meet and exceed what, at times, were competing expectations. It mattered not how I was feeling on the inside...*just get stuff done!* And stuff got done.

I became the queen of execution. You want it done and done fast? Send it to Shannon, she'll do it!

There's a huge sense of accomplishment when you can check the box and get the task done. Who doesn't love being the hero? I still feel this way today, but I've learned being the hero isn't all it's cracked up to be.

Unbeknownst to me, something was happening under the surface. With each new task, project, or team I agreed to be a part of, I paid a little less attention to myself and teeny tiny flickers of resentment began to burn. My only solution to the horrible feeling of resentment was to do the only thing I knew to do to feel that high again: achieve. And, since I was so service oriented, I needed to *help* others achieve in order to feel I had achieved too. That's what teachers do, right?

Looking back, I can clearly see how I developed this type of leadership, where my own sense of identity was baked into what I could produce for others.

Years later, when I helped start a leadership development organization whose platform is servant leadership, my first thought was, *I got this!*

Boy, was I wrong. And I carried this hero-complex with me into all my roles. First as a teacher, then a principal, then a Sales Coordinator in the corporate world, and again where I work today. To me this was servant leadership, but I was totally off. Thankfully, my current role exposed me to coaching that required me to do a lot of soul-searching and research. And it changed everything.

THE NEED FOR A MODEL

When I created my first leadership development program, I had no vision for our organization to focus on professional development as an overall strategic initiative.

None. I just wanted a program to help young professionals grow, while creating a new revenue stream for our struggling nonprofit. Based on both formal and anecdotal research, we built a new program on two primary tracks of learning: emotional intelligence and servant leadership.

The program was a huge hit, which made me believe once again, doing for others and producing are synonymous with servant leadership.

But by the end of year two of that very program, I learned we missed something really big. In the annual participant feedback survey, we learned what we were doing well but we also learned something huge was missing. The participants loved most of the program, but they craved a model for servant leadership.

We taught them *about* servant leadership; we covered the history, theories, and attributes, yes. But we left the *how* sort of fledgling out there with no direction. Warren Buffett, one of the most well-known and successful investors in the world, says that feedback is a gift and I have to agree. This desire for a model for servant leadership hit me right between the eyes. I actually couldn't believe I missed it!

While my motivation to find a model was to please our paying customers and execute on our mission, the end result brought me to a totally new place in my leadership and as a person; quite unexpectedly, I might add.

Finding a useful model for servant leadership would prove to be challenging; after all, we had based a large portion of our curriculum on research and information by those such as Robert Greenleaf, Ken Blanchard, and Russell and Stone. Robert Greenleaf, also known as The Father of Servant Leadership, founded what is considered the modern movement of servant leadership. In fact, his work was so influential that in 1985 The Center for Applied Ethics changed its name to the Greenleaf Center for Servant Leadership. Much of what is espoused today on the topic of servant leadership has its roots in Greenleaf's work. Ken Blanchard, born over thirty years later, went on to write dozens of books rooted in the tenants of servant leadership including the popular *One Minute Manager*. Even more recently, Robert F. Russell and A. Gregory Stone expanded the academic study of servant leadership in a popular white paper citing twenty attributes of servant leaders. (Robert F. Russell, A review of servant leadership attributes: developing a practical model 2002) Information and research around the topic of servant leadership abounds. These aforementioned thought leaders provide ample material for creating a training course of our own. And yet, distilling all of their thought leadership proved challenging.

OTHER MODELS

My assertion was simply this: there had to be a model out there-no need to reinvent the wheel. So, the research began. And guess what? There were many models. The models ranged from photos on Google with no real background available to complicated flowcharts requiring an Engineering degree to decipher.

The longer I looked, the more frustrated I became. That was until I revisited the work of Robert Greenleaf (known as the Father of Servant Leadership) and Russell and Stone. However, much of their work felt too academic for the program for which I wanted to use a model. The upside to this was I could benefit from their study and create a model of my own-from scratch-and I did.

Robert Greenleaf defines servant leadership as "a philosophy and a set of practices that enrich the lives of individuals, builds better organizations, and ultimately creates a more just and caring world." (Robert K. Greenleaf Center for Servant Leadership n.d.)

Using this definition, I realized our new model must implement philosophy (ways of thinking) and practices (ways of doing) too. A model only telling our participants what servant leaders should do is incomplete. The model must address how servant leaders think as well. But knowing how servant leaders think is still a *what. How can I learn to think like a servant leader?* That's the operating system of what would become our new model!

I call the model *CARE to Lead*, with CARE being an acronym: Connect, Align, Release and Engage. This book does not go into the CARE model but rather the operating system of the model. In other words, this book focuses on what the leader must think and feel in order to align themselves with the *doing* of the model more naturally and eventually, effortlessly.

MYTHS AND MISCONCEPTIONS

I knew I had been wrong about servant leadership so I felt the model must address common misunderstandings about servant leadership if it was to be useful. Apparently, I'm not the only one who has ever been wrong about servant leadership. Misconceptions regarding the style of leadership known as servant leadership persist. Here are just a few common ones along with my rebuttals:

Argument: Servant Leadership is "Too Internal"
This type of leader spends the majority of meetings caring only that everyone's work is meaningful while neglecting truly important details like profits and productivity.

Counter: Servant Leadership is an internal and external balance
Someone who truly understands servant leadership knows that you never meet the needs of one at the expense of another. In other words, a servant leader looks for the win/win for *all* stakeholders because they operate from a belief that it can be found. This means that a servant leader will never sacrifice profits in the name of "meaningful work" because the servant leader believes both can be achieved and will not move forward until they see how.

Argument: Growth Problems
Servant leaders cause a lack of motivation in their employees because they are always there to "baby" them and help with their work.

Counter: Growth Mindset

A servant leader does not chip in and help with the work and provide all the answers. This could not be further from the truth. A servant leader helps the employee by *not* doing the work for the employee while giving them the tools to do the work on their own. Why? Their ultimate concern is that the employee learns and grow.

And finally, ...

Argument: Possible Bullying

Servant Leaders are targets for manipulation. For example, an employee may feign not knowing how to perform a certain task, getting out of the responsibility, while the servant leader takes over. Conversely, one might argue that a servant leader could use the argument that since he helped the employee, the worker should respond by serving him.

Counter: Appropriate Boundaries

While manipulators certainly exist, the responsibility to draw boundaries lies in the servant leader's hands (and anyone's, for that matter). This is a victim stance that believes essentially that servant leaders are at the mercy of their followership. This paints a weak and wounded picture of the leader. Any leader can fail to draw appropriate boundaries. This is not unique to any leadership style, but rather a problem of another sort.

Traditional leaders can tend to lead by manipulation. In true servant leadership, manipulation does not come into play.

Between these misconceptions and the wide array of information available on the topic of servant leadership, a model needed to emerge.

As I revisited Greenleaf's definition of servant leadership, something still bothered me. Nowhere in Greenleaf's definition or these comparisons do we see the servant leader developing themselves. Maybe this point is inferred, but I believed it was worth calling out. After all, how can I serve others and help them develop if I am suffering, in need of development and depleted? Like me, leaders believe if they are creating success in their businesses, the internal frustrations and pain are just a part of the package. They are not. There must be a balance or ebb and flow of sorts. There absolutely had to be a win/win in the model. Literally win/win must be at the core of the model. And so "Everybody Wins" was added to the core.

Looking at the attributes of servant leadership once again, you'll find vast information. I chose to stick with the academics once again. Greenleaf, Spears, and Russell and Stone became my focus. Larry Spears (1998), CEO of the Greenleaf Center, studied Greenleaf's works in depth and determined that Robert Greenleaf utilized ten major attributes of servant leadership.

The ten major attributes of servant leadership a la Greenleaf are: Listening, Empathy, Healing, Awareness, Persuasion, Conceptualization, Foresight, Stewardship, Commitment to the growth of people and Building community.

Spears explained however, these attributes were in no way exhaustive and that other attributes identified in Greenleaf's work could reveal up to twenty in alignment with Greenleaf's writings.

In 2002, Russell and Stone's white paper on the *twenty attributes* of servant leadership was published. This publication provided an in-depth description of the attributes of servant leaders. The twenty attributes (Fig. 1) were separated into Functional and Accompanying. Functional attributes are those that represent characteristics of servant leadership, while Accompanying attributes can augment the Functional attributes. Each attribute was given a

SERVANT LEADERSHIP ATTRIBUTES
Russel & Stone, 2002

Functional
Vision
Honesty
Integrity
Trust
Service
Modeling
Pioneering
Appreciation of others
Empowerment

Accompanying
Communication
Credibility
Competence
Stewardship
Visibility
Influence
Persuasion
Listening
Encouragement
Teaching
Delegation

Figure 1

14

specific purpose and definition to help the reader know potentially how to implement the idea into action. (Robert F. Russell 2002) It was this particular resource I used for the first two years of that leadership development program.

As you can imagine, implementing all twenty attributes into one's own leadership style presents a challenge, thus the need for a simpler model. The work became figuring out how to take those attributes and simplify them into four or five steps.

The process of creating a simplified model from these attributes went through dozens of iterations, rewrites, and revisions. I'm actually chuckling right now as I look at all my old research and click through early versions of the model. The acronym CARE never changed, but the words for each letter changed many times. This process of changing and editing was arduous at best but mostly aggravating. I suppose it shouldn't be easy to distill twenty attributes into a 4-step model. And it wasn't.

THE MODEL

The CARE to Lead model is an acronym: Connect, Align, Release and Engage. There is a direct connection from each of the twenty servant leadership attributes to one or more of the letters in the model. This model simplifies servant leadership into four big, simple (but not easy) steps that create a *virtuous* cycle of commitment while building competence. And, I wanted a more digestible model for my workshops. My desire was to honor the research of thought leaders like Robert Greenleaf and Russell and Stone without turning my servant leadership workshops into heavy academic lectures. Figure 2 shows each step of the model with the associated servant leader attributes that were used and considered when creating the model, CARE to Lead.

Servant Leadership Attributes

CONNECT	ALIGN	RELEASE	ENGAGE
Communication	Vision	Service	Honesty
Visibility	Pioneering	Modeling	Appreciation of Others
Listening	Stewardship	Empowerment	Encouragement
Integrity	Persuasion	Competence	Teaching
Trust	Credibility	Delegation	
	Influence		

Figure 2

The CARE to Lead Model

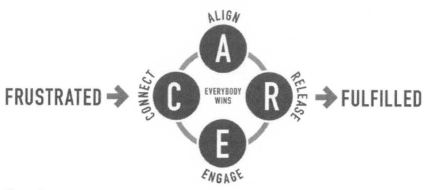

FRUSTRATED → [CONNECT] C [ALIGN A] EVERYBODY WINS [ENGAGE E] R [RELEASE] → FULFILLED

Figure 3

While this book is not about the CARE model, the mindsets are derived from the model. For each step in CARE, there is a core mindset that when embraced and practiced, can help the individual to begin to embody the related attributes as listed above. The bulk of this book is dedicated to addressing the core mindset for each step in the CARE model, plus one additional mindset; thus, five mindsets.

I truly believe if I tell a willing leader what to do to be a better servant leader, he or she will grow, but the growth may be surface and even short-lived. But, what if instead I could show someone how to change their own thinking so as to more effortlessly embody the servant leader attributes?

And how this embodiment can be done with simple shifts in thinking? I like that idea a lot. They might grow in a way that brings lasting change.

Inspired by Robert Greenleaf, I created a definition of servant leadership that leaves room for the servant leader to consider their own interests (needs and wants). In the grand picture of win/win, no one is left out. That definition is as follows:

> "Servant Leadership is a style in which the leader balances the interests of others and self while relentlessly pursuing a win for all stakeholders. These leaders seek to enrich lives, build better organizations, and care for one another."

What I love most about this definition is the recognition of self. I cannot give from an empty place. I cannot give what I do not possess. I was motivated to include this in the definition because of my old way of thinking and believing which was this: If I serve until I'm empty, then I've *really* served.

This isn't true. Running on empty means I'm trying to give what I do not possess. This makes no sense. We cannot relentlessly pursue wins for all if we are not winning too. Period.

2
PERSPECTIVE: LEADERSHIP IS AN INSIDE JOB

There is a difference between having the title of a leader and actually leading people in way that creates followers. But how does a leader create this kind of follow-ship? How does a leader *get the people*?

Some have said the term "servant leadership" is a paradox. Maybe. Or maybe we've perverted the connotation of the world leader? Leaders have followers, yes. But how those followers are obtained and how they feel while following matters. The servant leader cares about this very thing, understanding they are not responsible for other people's feelings but play a role in the environments they create.

Furthermore, servant leaders are not motivated by being the boss, rather by developing others. The motivation to be in charge is to make a difference in the lives of individuals, communities, and organizations. A positive difference. The motivation is not to have the people but "having the people" is the result. Very interesting. So back to my question. How does a leader *get the people*?

R.E.A.L.

The only way I know to answer this question is through my own experience, by evaluating the most beloved and effective leaders in my life personally and that I have access to publicly. I think of people who are humble, truthful, have integrity, and engage with others. These are also leaders who seem to have a full life outside of work. They spend time with their families, travel, contribute to the community, and lend their talent to nonprofits. These are all-around friendly and great-to-be-around people. To me these leaders are R.E.A.L.

Relatable. Empathetic. Authentic. Loving.

Just think about those words for a few minutes. I'll break them down on the next pages but based on your own understanding of what they mean, are you *R.E.A.L.*? How often? How well? Being a R.E.A.L. leader is a tall order.

This is why I believe leadership is an inside job. Being real is work. We are born pure and unfettered by circumstances but eventually things happen in our lives and we develop coping mechanisms-some good, some not so good. When those same coping mechanisms make their way into our adult lives and leadership, they can become maladaptive and cause pain. Because of this shared human experience, I think the exact opposite of "real" is what most of us get from leaders, and the R.E.A.L. leaders are as common as the mythical unicorn.

There are those who say no one can truly change at their core. I disagree.

There are certain situations and triggers that simply do not bother me anymore. I have changed. What about you? Are you the same person you were five, ten, or twenty years ago? I hope not. I hope you have evolved in at least one area of your life.

My hope is that we become better versions of ourselves as we learn and grow and also that we pick up new tools while we put a few others down. Most of us discovered tools in our childhood for dealing with whatever circumstances came our way. Then, on the path to maturity, probably learned some hard lessons about which of those tools no longer work in adulthood. When we refuse to put down those old tools, dysfunction reigns.

When I was a teen and into my twenties, I helped people a lot. I volunteered, went to youth group, accepted extra projects at work, and went out of my way to help friends. The only problem was, I resented most of it. Externally, I was doing good, right? Helping is good! But, as I entered my thirties and resentments grew, I began to learn about my motivations. I saw how some childhood self-protective tools didn't work anymore; how my motivations for helping were really from a childhood need to be accepted. I learned that doing for someone in hopes they do for me in return is really manipulation. I had to put that tool down. Now, I only help if I want to help and can do so without the need of approval or needing to be liked. It's simple to say, but it is something I have to be aware of regularly.

I have changed at my core through awareness of where I was; how it was hurtful to me, getting a picture of where I wanted to be; then learning and a process to get there by changing my mindset.

Change is possible for you too.

PROGRESS

Whenever I talk to people about making a change or hear others talk about improving their life, I hear a lot about striking a balance. If you believe balance tends to refer to something being even, then I have some bad news for you: I don't believe balance is achievable or even realistic. More realistic to me, is the idea of progress. Where am I today? Where do I want to be in the future? How do I get there?

When I look at my life up until now, my life is marked by progress, not balance. I hope yours is too. Admittedly, there are times I have been a better wife than an Executive Director. Plenty of times I was a better mom than a wife. And sometimes I'm barely hanging on in all but one area. Balance? No.

I have also experienced seasons of bliss. A season of bliss is when I felt like I was hitting on all eight cylinders in all areas of my life. These are times when there's peace in my soul, the words flow easily on paper, money in the bank, my kids are happy, my business is growing, and the husband is fulfilled at work. But those moments have been few and far between.

I don't know about you, but things going well in my life tend to give me a false sense of security and expectation if I'm not mindful. When I'm on the mountain top, I feel like I'm always going to be there. But when I'm in the valley, I feel like I'm always going to be there as well.

While I'm not suggesting the lowering of expectations to the point of apathy or lack of achievement, I am suggesting the idea of balance is simply made up, and furthermore, creates more frustration than fulfillment. If I am expecting that my life is "balanced," when clearly this is not possible most of the time, I'm going to be disappointed most of the time.

Instead, I find it much more powerful to embrace the idea that I can revel in the few times in my life where I felt like I was *killing it* and celebrate those times, really enjoy them. But then the rest of the time, accept that life is more about progress, seven days a week. Life is part sweet and part bitter. I expect to get good and bad in life and know that just like the bad times don't last, neither do the good. Both make up the whole of my life and both make the other possible. The contrast of the ups and downs of life are what make this whole damn experience such an adventure!

Balance is not the goal. Progress is. This allows me to be content in the disharmony and the lack of balance, understanding it means I'm improving.

My hope for you is that you can get honest about where you are today *on the inside*, paint a picture of a desired destination, and chart a workable path to close the gap.

R.E.A.L. LEADERS

Let's break down R.E.A.L. I pulled most of these straight out of the dictionary to get started.

Relatable

Being relatable means, you establish a social or sympathetic relationship with a person or a thing. R.E.A.L. leaders need to be connected socially with what they do and who they lead. This doesn't necessarily mean you are getting together for beers every Thursday after work. This is not about friendships per se. The social aspect does, however, relate to being knowable, vulnerable, approachable, and available. And while I won't go into the depth of each of those words, I find them adequate to describe what essentially could be wrapped up by saying to be human, and to be warm.

All too many leaders are seen as aloof, separate, distant, and overly serious. These leaders are not perceived as being relatable. You cannot relate to someone you are distant from. You cannot truly lead if you do not understand and are not understood. It is very difficult to understand from a distance.

Traditional leadership often embraces an "us and them" mentality, a top-down approach to leadership where the leader is so far removed from those they lead and not only *not* relatable but seen as being out of touch.

Being relatable is not about being the cool or hip leader. Being relatable is also not about giving into all the whims and wants of those being led. No.

Being relatable means the leader takes the time to know and care about the wants and needs of those being led; not so they can cater to them but so that they can understand and have better informed decisions. Without this knowing and being known, decisions are made in a vacuum with little or no input from those whom the decision affects, with even less effort put into explaining the rationale. This does not demonstrate a social connection to those who are led.

Being relatable and connected socially to those you lead does not mean everyone gets what they want. It does mean the leader cares enough to *know* what others want. Every person who has ever led anything knows; the leader cannot serve all the wants of every person involved in the business. Any leader who attempts this will certainly burn out. But a relatable leader isn't afraid to know what's important to those they lead and explain why decisions were made, even if the decision meant not every need was met. This R.E.A.L. leader explains their thought process because they focus on people first, coming from a belief that people matter.

Empathetic

To be empathetic is to have a psychological identification with the feelings, thoughts, or attitudes of others. Notice I didn't say emotional over-identification. Being empathetic doesn't necessarily mean that if others around you are sad you are sad too. Or, if people around you are angry, you must become angry too.

The psychological identification is that you care enough to recognize when these feelings and thoughts are occurring and call them out in a peaceful and caring way so as to connect with people and make a safe space for their reactions. I might even go a step further and say that the psychological identification is actually a recognition of what is happening with the other person, and *what is happening is separate from you*. This is not about reacting to what other people think and feel. This is about knowing, allowing, and accepting that other people have their own thoughts and feelings about all things and as a leader, you can make room for those things without being threatened. And, you can remain relatable while identifying with parts of you that have felt the same way...there's that human understanding again!

This can be difficult for leaders. We want to fix. Empathy doesn't need to fix; it only holds space and creates safety.

Authentic

The next way R.E.A.L. leaders connect meaningfully to others is by remaining authentic. But authenticity isn't as easy as just 'be yourself'.

Yes, being authentic has to do with representing one's true nature and/or beliefs. There are many definitions for authentic in the dictionary with words that include unique and original, and while all of those are accurate, I chose to home in on this one in particular because I felt it created an interesting take on the whole process of viewing leadership as an inside job. How so?

Well, you can be a totally authentic jerk! If your true nature is to be mean, spiteful and negative and that's how you show up every day, then you are, in fact, being authentic. Part of this process is looking at your true nature now and if you desire a different nature. How do you know if you may want to rewrite part of your truer nature?

Your results.

If your authentic self is holding you back in some way, it may be time to change. My true nature was service to a fault and resulted in growing resentments inside of me. I needed this to change and I wanted to create authentic change-I wanted my true nature to change. Yours can change too if you are ready.

Loving

Asking leaders to be loving can seem too soft, too squishy. This isn't a romantic love, as I'm sure you already know. It's more about motivation.

Are you motivated from a place of choices or a "rock and a hard place"? Are you motivated from a place of opportunity or limitations? Are you motivated from a place of abundance or scarcity? Are you motivated from a place of love or fear?

Listen, leadership can be scary. It takes great courage to just get out of bed and face the challenges of the day. But as long as we face those challenges from a position of fear, we are missing out on so many choices and opportunities! How?

When we are in fear, our minds literally shut down options. Our minds want the fastest path to safety and sometimes in work (and in life), the fastest path is not the path that is best. But when we are fearful, we can't evaluate the options because *we cannot see them*. Any time we make decisions from a place of fear, we cannot also make the decisions from a place of love.

A loving leader intentionally slows down to consider their choices, opportunities, and most importantly, "What is the best for as many people as possible?"

I know the concern here. The concern is that risks won't be evaluated. But this isn't true.

I'm suggesting that a loving leader *starts* with the biggest possible net of ideas, solutions and options, all from a place of love and opportunity. Then, that leader employs their reasoning skills and trusted advisors to evaluate the risks and benefits of all their choices. This way, the leader is lovingly considering all who may be affected before making a choice and can reasonably defend and explain a conclusion.

Does it take more time? Yes. Is it worth it? Absolutely yes.

TRUTH

I'd be remiss if I didn't touch on a specific topic within the idea of being a R.E.A.L. leader, and that is the topic of truth.

Edward R. Murrow, an American broadcast journalist, says, "To be persuasive, you must be believable; to be believable, you must be credible; and to be credible, you must be truthful."

But what is truth?

Depending on the usage of the word, truth could mean a few things. Religious scholars for ages have claimed to possess *the absolute truth*, usually a truth represented by historic leaders, sacred texts, and visions revealed. Others have made broad statements, like, "Whatever is truth to you is truth." I get that too. I stand firm that if you believe a thing, to you, that thing is true.

Then there's this notion of universal truth: something that is true all the time, everywhere, for everyone. That seems pretty absolute and broad all at the same time.

So rather than argue about which approach is the best, I'll share a few subtle ways we dishonor R.E.A.L. leadership by skirting truth and honesty.

I'll offer up my own mistake as the first example. Remember my former version of servant leadership where I just helped everyone all the time? You know, the kind that made me mad and resentful? Where do you think those resentments came from?

They came from unmet expectations. I do something for you and then expect you to do something for me. Except I don't tell you this expectation. My doing for you was actually a selfish and dishonest way of trying to get my own needs met, under the veil of service. We've all done it. Let's stop.

Here's another example: how about pretending to know everything in an effort to seem more knowledgeable, put together, or connected than we are? I was once at an event where I met several new people. There was a woman there who, when asked if she knew so-and-so or had seen such-and-such, etc., would always respond in the affirmative. "Oh yes, that film was amazing"; "Oh my, he is a fantastic leader, yes I know him" and on and on. I thought, wow, she is just super connected.

As the weekend rolled on, I noticed a couple attendees listening to some her claims of knowing this person and that person, would ask her follow up questions as a result. It became embarrassingly apparent that she did not know these people at all. She was "mistaken" about almost all of the connections she claimed to have.

It seemed she needed others to believe she was more knowledgeable and connected than maybe she was and could not bring herself to admit she did not know something or someone.

Listen, it's okay to not know. It's okay to not know people, movies, events, award or even current events. And as a leader, it's okay to not know all the answers in the face of questions from those you lead.

Saying you know something when you don't is lying. It's dishonest. It's not real; in fact, it's pretty fake. Let's stop this too.

Finally, R.E.A.L. leaders who are committed to truth enter regularly into honest self-assessment. In other words, R.E.A.L. leaders don't get mixed up in self-delusion.

In this book you will get the opportunity to informally self-assess. Taking formal assessments are helpful and bring many insights, but I'd like you to figure out how to assess on your own. I want you to get used to and comfortable with taking a daily inventory of your innermost motivations and resultant outcomes. Only in that self-awareness can you decide if you are ready for change or not. Your willingness to change is all that is needed to get started on this journey.

I encourage you to open up to the fact that you may be wrong about a few things. You may be wrong about leadership, servant leadership, and how you're showing up as a leader. Just practice saying this out loud:

I may be wrong.

Go ahead-say it again. *I may be wrong.*

Because here's the good news: once you're wrong, you can learn and grow. Listen folks, if you aren't wrong, there's nothing to change. If there's nothing to change, there's no growth. We've all heard it said, admitting you have a problem is the first step, right? Admitting you're wrong creates the vacuum, the space that needs filled with new knowledge, new ideas, and new mindsets-and new results.

I know there are fears associated with admitting you don't know something, asking for help, self-assessing, and working on your motivations for serving others. Honestly, I'd be worried if you weren't a little doubtful. All I ask at this point is that you remain willing to engage in this process. Don't worry about chapter six or ten. Just take this one step at a time.

At this point, we've looked at what we mean by servant leadership. We have further honed great leadership into R.E.A.L. leadership. You may even start to feel a tinge inside, telling you about some changes you may need to make. Try to suspend the temptation to make those determinations just yet, as we work on some simple ways to self-assess where you are today versus where servant leadership sits out in the future for you.

3
EVALUATION: HOW DO I MEASURE UP?

Once I learned more about servant leadership, I wanted to jump right in to becoming one. I saw servant leadership as my answer, but I didn't understand fully why. I only knew what I had learned up until this point was attractive to me. I gained enough knowledge that I knew I wasn't *there*. I knew I wasn't a servant leader deep down. Identifying a true need for growth does require understanding the desired destination. In my case, my destination was becoming a servant leader, and specifically, a more mindful leader, and I found the challenge of honing that towards servant leadership very appealing. But unless I evaluated where I was in comparison, I had no way of knowing specifically where I needed the most work. To be clear: I knew that by comparison I was not where I wanted or needed to be; however, I didn't have any specifics as to what I was missing. At least, not yet.

Evaluating where you are as a leader and as a person on the inside compared to where you want to be doesn't have to be a complicated process. Can it be made complex? Yes. Are formal tools helpful? Sure. But I want this to be accessible to those who may or may not have access to such tools.

Please know I love and respect formal assessments. Actually, I'm kind of a nerd about them because they tell me about one of my favorite subjects: me! There is some sort of validation that comes when I sit down to read and understand my results from formal assessment tools. To me, it's kind of fun. The gift of feedback cannot be brushed aside, and I encourage anyone to pursue any and all types of assessments that are available and relevant to their life and work. My only caution is this: assessments only help you know more *about yourself*; they do not help you *know yourself.*

Learning to informally self-assess is a tool you can take with you, regardless of you or your employer's ability to provide an assessment for you. Are there assessments that can reveal to you what you may not be able to discover on your own? Absolutely. And, with some added self-awareness, there are steps you can take to create a little more intellectual honesty for yourself on an ongoing basis. But if we're limited to formal assessment tools for our growth, we may miss out on taking ongoing responsibility for our own development.

ASSESS BY COMPARISON

Understanding what servant leadership is helps to create a desired future state. Further awareness can be found by contrasting servant leadership to other forms of leadership. When I started reading about servant leadership, my initial reaction was, *Oh, that's me. I got this!* But, when I read about other leadership styles *and* the mindsets associated with them, what I realized was that I agreed with servant leadership cognitively, but I wasn't actually executing on the *behaviors*. This dissonance caused me to question why. Why, when I learn a new thing, do I not embody the new thing, even when I intellectually agree with the thing? You'd think change would be automatic in this instance, but it was not for me.

In my opinion, this is one of the reasons we don't

change. We mentally ascend to an idea, but that idea isn't actually a part of how we show up. In other words, that mental idea has not made the eight-inch drop into our heart, into our very being. What I had to realize was the concepts associated with servant leadership were not a part of my everyday choices and actions even though I agreed with them. Curiosity around this incongruence is what created a thirst for understanding the impact of mindset on behavior.

Styles of Leadership

To more fully assess where my leadership stood in comparison to servant leadership, I needed to look at other leadership styles. I compared what I was learning about servant leadership to more of the traditional leadership I had experienced thus far in my life. The chart in Fig. 4 helps contrast the two styles. This kind of distinction provides some broad brush stroke descriptions for each style. Then, I'll provide a more extensive look at several other leadership styles.

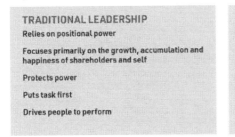
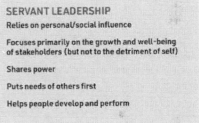

Figure 4

There are three main categories I see when considering the differences between the traditional and the servant leader. Those are differences in the use of delegation, communication of vision and wielding of power.

Delegation

Both a traditional and servant leader understands the importance of delegation from a practical standpoint. The leader cannot do all the work (although many try). But the servant leader thoughtfully delegates meaningful work to others based on others' development needs and capabilities. The servant leader is thinking, "What does this person need to grow? What tasks, projects, and challenges can I delegate to help this person meet and exceed what they believe is possible?" To the servant leader, delegation is not just about getting stuff off their own plate, it is about helping another person learn, grow and develop.

Vision

Most leaders agree, a vision and mission must be communicated to those who are led. The mistake some traditional leaders make is in trying to simply *tell* people about the vision for the organization, believing that by telling, they are aligning people to that vision. Communicating vision is a very small part of casting a vision. The real work comes when it is time to align others to that vision and craft values and behaviors supportive of that same vision. Traditional leaders simply expect these things to magically happen and then are often surprised when they do not.

The servant leader takes the time to know their people and their higher purpose in life and to connect their higher purpose to the purpose of the organization. This servant leader views vision as a creative process, understanding that individuals connect and align to a vision in unique ways. The main vision is the same for all, but how each person connects to that vision and draws meaning from it is different for all.

The servant leader knows that aligning purpose to vision is good for people. This kind of alignment brings a deeper degree of job satisfaction, even if passion about their actual job is low. A more satisfied employee is more engaged and productive. More on this in chapter six. Let's look at one more.

Power

We've all heard people in authority say things like, "Because I said so!" Or maybe it's been said in our homes from our parents. Have you had a leader or boss talk this way too? I have.

The reliance on positional power is a traditional leader's go-to move. Dependence on positional power is rooted many things like fear, ignorance and lack of care. If caused by fear, typically this leader is driving performance. Why? Performance means we hit goals and make money and this leader has put their faith in those outcomes. If caused by ignorance, the leader simply doesn't know better. Maybe they were brought up to believe a leader should be followed and obeyed simply because they are the leader. Or maybe they simply do not know how to influence in more formative ways like through connection and social influence. And if caused by lack of care...well this leader may know better and simply doesn't give a shit. I've met those and fortunately, they are few and far between.

The servant leader relies on influence and social connection because they understand connection is a basic need of all human beings. The servant leader thinks about how people need to be connected to as well. There is no need for fear-based leadership because the servant leader has adopted a mindset that fear is limiting, and they do not have to control people or outcomes. Ignorance is reduced, as the servant leader is committed to becoming and remaining aware of the blank spots in their leadership; they are committed to continuous personal improvement. And they give a shit.

In these three examples, do you see how the servant leader puts people first, just in different ways?

The overriding theme when comparing servant leadership to traditional leadership is motivation. The motivation of the servant leader is putting people first. Putting people first means the servant leader is thinking about others first (without ignoring self). But "others first" is just too simple and generic. Look at the Traditional versus Servant Leadership chart. Where are you?

Now let's look at some other leadership styles. While I don't claim this list is exhaustive, I believe it covers most leadership styles and/or our experiences with leaders. Please note: while servant leadership is technically a leadership style, my opinion is that a mindset shift is needed to truly servant lead.

The first time I ever presented to a group of teachers on servant leadership, I provided the chart in Fig. 5. One of the teachers interrupted and said I'd left out one leadership style: situational leadership. He went on to say, "Situational Leadership is the best kind of leadership because it takes into account what the other person needs...isn't that servant leadership?" And you know what? The gentleman had a great point.

While situational leadership is in essence serving those we lead by intentionally showing up for others in ways that they need (both in support and direction), the style itself does not address the mindset of the leader-at least not directly. According to the extensive work of Ken Blanchard Companies on situational leadership, the situational leader must be able to diagnose where each person is on their team from two main perspectives: the need for support and the need for direction. (The Ken Blanchard Companies 2017) Then, the situational leader provides the appropriate amount of support and direction based on that developmental level in an effort to build both competence and commitment on the job. It is a wonderful model and one I am certified to teach. That's how much I believe in it.

However, the main difference I see is that servant leadership (as defined by me in this book) is just as concerned with a leader's *motivations and emotions* which influence how they choose to show up, not just that they *behave* in a certain way. In other words, servant leadership is *concerned with the experience of the leader while leading,* not just the actions towards those being led, because the internal experience of the leader creates an external experience for their team. A final note on situational leadership-to me, situational leadership provides the tactical application of servant leadership.

This is why I believe a servant leaders mindset book is needed. To effectively show up for our teams and communities in ways that take their needs into account, we must operate from the appropriate mindset to match.

I can tell you all the ways a servant leader should

behave, like what strategies and tactics they use to more fully servant lead. But if you are still miserable, full of anxiety and conflict while leading, you haven't learned the true nature of servant leadership. Yes, leadership is challenging and, on some days, downright heartbreaking. I am not promising rainbows and butterflies here. But great leadership shouldn't cost you your peace of mind.

There are pros and cons for each of the common leadership styles. Finding out which style works best in any given situation is definitely important. However, I believe if more people can first and foremost learn to embrace servant leadership as their preferred mindset, that servant leader mindset will impact *how* they utilize the other types of leadership styles in different situations. The "how" is important.

The chart (Fig. 5) gives a very quick understanding of each leadership style. Notice there are many parts of the pros which actually fall within the attributes of servant leadership. For example, the Charismatic Leader is marked by being *visionary*; the Laissez-Faire Leader is primarily concerned with unleashing potential (this can be done effectively via *delegation*); and finally, Transactional. This style harnesses efficiency, which takes a considerable degree of *competence*.

Now think about yourself in comparison to those styles. Do you see yourself showing up more heavily in one style versus another? Do you identify with the pros or cons of that style or both? You'll know if you are out of balance when you can observe and feel the cons with those you lead. Take time to write some notes on each on just your cursory observations of self.

Leadership Style	Pros	Cons
Autocratic Dictates policies/procedures; decides goals; controls activities; no meaningful participation from subordinates	Efficient	Staff resentment; difficult to sustain
Bureaucratic Fixed official rules; hierarchy; system for management; Great for production-oriented environments where creativity and innovation isn't needed.	Effective; Consistent	Demoralizing; change difficult
Charismatic Leadership based on personality, charisma; leader still owns everything	Visionary; Energizing	Depends heavily on the leader; lack of staff 'ownership'
Democratic Team guided by a leader	Team engaged and contributing; work of high quality can result	Takes time
Laissez-Faire All rights/power given to the employees	Unleashes the potential of capable, experienced employees	Leader's strengths not be fully utilized; less capable staff not guided
Task-Oriented Leader focused on specific **tasks** to reach specific goals	Effective; leader plays a key role in planning and executing	Staff feel unappreciated, because they aren't considered
People-Oriented Leader focused on well-being, motivation and satisfaction of team	Good for teamwork, creative collaboration and staff satisfaction	Task completion/goal attainment can suffer, if taken to extremes
Transactional Managerial; leader promotes compliance through reward and punishment; focused on role of supervision, organization and group performance	Work is done reliably; staff adheres to standards	Staff lacks true buy-in, feel under-valued; Stifles creativity and drive
Transformational Leaders works w/employees to ID needed change, jointly dev. vision; guides change through inspiration and gets things done with committed members of the group	Visionary style used to motivate and inspire; gets things done via delegation	Needs effective managers to ensure creation of plans and implementation
Servant Leadership Focus moves from the tasks, vision and change of org to finding out what employee's highest needs are and working to fulfill those; based on org values versus org goals. Hiring based on values versus goals as well.	Staff involved and feel cared for; organization values are clear	Can put the leader at a competitive disadvantage in some settings

Figure 5

THE LEADER UNDER STRESS

All of us want to believe we put people first. But do we? When you get scared or stressed at work, what is your default reaction? Is your reaction to protect self, avoid people and demand performance? If so, you may lean more towards traditional leadership when things get tough.

I believe most leaders are doing the best they can with the knowledge and development they have at any given moment. Those leaders have the ability to put people first when they are calm, and everything is going their way. The reason I ask about your reaction when stressed or scared is because what we do in those times reveals who we really are; or at least a big part of who we are. And, if we are stressed and scared a lot at work, guess what? We aren't showing up as our best selves very often. Much of leadership is stress. As leaders, we experience ambiguity, conflict, and difficulty on a daily basis. What if you could learn to remain as calm in the tough times as you do when work is all rainbows and butterflies?

When I first entered into my own servant leadership journey, I realized the mindset of servant leadership required a very high level of awareness. That new awareness started with an assessment tool that was used when I had my first-ever executive coaching experience and the tool is called the Energy Leadership Index (ELI) Assessment. This assessment tool has been validated for over twenty years by Dr. Bruce Schneider, who is the founder of the Institute for Professional Excellence in Coaching, otherwise known as IPEC.

IPEC asserts that leaders engage in anabolic (creative, constructive) and catabolic (destructive, tense) energy. The ELI tool measures this energy. More interestingly, the energy expended can be measured in both ideal and stressful circumstances. Thus, the person taking the assessment receives two scores: their energy level under stress (catabolic) and their energy level when not under stress (anabolic). Generally speaking, the lower and less frequent your catabolic energy, the higher and more frequent your anabolic energy (Energy Leadership 2019). Taking part in this assessment, understanding my results, and receiving coaching as a result created a new leadership consciousness for me.

Now, if the term "consciousness" is kind of weird to you, try thinking of it this way: internal knowledge of your surroundings, thoughts, interpretations, motivations, etc. When someone is more conscious of these types of things, they can make more choices about their actions. When someone is less conscious, fewer choices. Why? You cannot make choices about things you are unaware of.

The results of the ELI help the leader become more conscious of how they show up and what influences the way they show up. I've done my very best to simplify the levels of this model and explain them here as another step for you to self-assess. There is a correlation to servant leadership-I'll get to that soon!

	Core Thought	Core Feeling	Action
1	VICTIM	APATHY	LETHARGY
2	CONFLICT	ANGER	DEFIANCE
3	RESPONSIBILITY	FORGIVENESS	COOPERATION
4	CONCERN	COMPASSION	SERVICE
5	RECONCILIATION	PEACE	ACCEPTANCE
6	SYNTHESIS	JOY	WISDOM
7	NON-JUDGMENT	ABSOLUTE PASSION	CREATION

Figure 6

The chart in Fig. 6 provides the core thought feeling and action at each level-these terms come from ELI. Then, I've provided everyday layman's terms to describe each level in my own words.

Level 1: Victim Consciousness

You can sum up victim consciousness with "I lose." at the core. Someone who spends a lot of time in Level 1 is almost never conscious of being in this state. In fact, most of those with victim mindsets will rail against the idea that they are victims.

Obvious examples of victim thinking are easy to identify. The subtle victim thoughts are what I'm interested in pointing out. Here are a few statements that come to mind:

"I can't tell our controller he's being mean to the other associates. He'll quit!"

"If I hold people accountable, they will get mad."

"I can't tell my client they can't be late! They will find a new consultant."

"This is just the way I am!"

Victim thinking is marked by a feeling of apathy that leads to lethargy. The victim-thinker believes they are trapped and have no choices. The end result is no action taken. It's easy to call a person victim-minded who acts woe-is-me, but how often do you fail to take action by pinning yourself into a corner? That's victim thinking too.

Any time you're not willing to take responsibility or recognize your part or your responsibility in something, you're playing the victim.

Level 2: Conflict Consciousness

Those in Conflict Consciousness are a bit more active than those stuck in victim consciousness. Their mantra is "You lose."

While there are extreme examples of conflict thinking resulting in things like physical violence, that's not what we're talking about as far as leadership goes. This "you lose" mentality is one born of anger that results in defiance, and defiance can show up in many ways. From the person who simply cannot turn that weekly report in on time to the person who will not comply with workplace rules, the defiance is evident.

But defiance can also play out in ways less obvious.

The most common way I've seen it played out is in the refusal to employ discretionary effort. This refusal isn't an inability to give discretionary effort, no. I'm referring to the person who could exceed expectations but refuses to in an effort to punish someone. This is insidious because they usually perform their job satisfactorily, but they withhold their gold standard performance *on purpose*. This person is mad about something and what's sad is that they are largely unaware of the harm they do to themselves in the process.

Is all conflict bad? Absolutely not. Some conflict is necessary even. This is about the core thought, feeling, and action of a person-the internal environment-and what that person is doing with the conflict they encounter. We all experience conflict, but it is a choice to respond in anger. I had no idea it was possible to feel conflict, become aware of my anger and then choose a new way. It can be done. We don't have to get stuck in Conflict Consciousness if we don't want to.

Level 1 and 2 are almost always damaging to self and others, which is the key differentiator between Level 1 and 2 and the rest of the Levels.

Level 3: Coping Consciousness

Coping Consciousness is all about "I win but I hope you win too." This mindset doesn't mean this person wants you to lose, they are simply focused on what they need to do to survive first. Why? This person's core thought is responsibility, probably because harmony is important to them. Their harmonious responsibility creates feelings of forgiveness for wrongs done (instead of anger) which results in cooperation.

A person primarily in Coping Consciousness is more than likely a reliable worker who gets along with others, gets their job done, and maintains a general care for others. In other words, "I know what I need. I'm going to get it, and I'm aware that you need to feel okay too, at least some of the time, so I will try not to meet my needs at the expense of yours." This recognition that we both have needs results primarily in cooperation.

Make no mistake, there are plenty of people who look cooperative outwardly by doing their job but inside are angry and defiant. These individuals are simply afraid of losing their job. These individuals are actually in Conflict Consciousness. Remember, the focus of this tool is looking at what's inside, what motivates you. If you're feeling angry but pretending, you're not through cooperation, you're smack dab in the middle of Level 2 still.

Level 4: Giving Consciousness

Level 4 takes a dramatic shift and says, "You win!" Someone who shows up primarily in Giving Consciousness is concerned for others first. This concern creates feelings of compassion which result in powerful service to others and even the world! Some might say this is servant leadership- but not so fast.

The "unhealthy" Level 4 is getting out of balance and a person in Giving Consciousness who is out of balance is at risk of devolving into Level 2. How so? When you do for others at your own expense and give until you are depleted, you will end up resentful. Resentments are just a form of anger (conflict).

Level 4 is helpful for getting out of Level 1 and 2 in a couple ways. First, when we find ourselves in victim thinking, we stop instead, and get concerned first for ourselves. What needs did we have that were left unmet? What corners have we placed ourselves in that are unnecessary? This jump to self-concern will get our brains out of victim mode.

Second, when we find ourselves at odds with others and situations (conflict), instead we can get concerned about them, get curious. If, instead of being angry that Karen didn't say "Hi" to me yesterday, I got curious and began to be concerned about her and *why* she didn't acknowledge me, I'd be a lot less likely to be angry.

I know it sounds too simple, but it isn't easy. Our brains are wired to default to these levels and for many of us, that default happens the majority of the time.

Yes, servant leadership begins here but I do not believe servant leadership can live solely at Level 4.

Level 5: Everybody Wins Consciousness

Level 5 says, "We all win, or we don't play." This leader is no longer thinking about someone losing at all! This leader sees opportunity for all and believes the win can be found. An Everybody Wins attitude may seem lofty or even impossible. In fact, when I talk to leaders about Level 5 Consciousness, the response is typically, 'Yeah, right!' I completely understand this reaction and at the same time I insist Level 5 is possible.

Striving for Level 5 then is more about the internal commitment to looking for the win for as many people as possible as often as possible; the commitment to evaluating as many choices as possible, whenever possible, without defaulting to win:lose or worse, lose:lose.

In my experience, servant leadership is an intricate balance of Level 4 and 5 because Level 4 is the linchpin for getting out of Level 1 and 2 and Level 5 ensures the win is being sought for all, including self.

The CARE to Lead Model and subsequently this book strives for a level 4 - 5. While I know Levels 4 and 5 are a tall order, as a servant leader, I believe these levels can be attained more frequently with practice. And here's what's interesting: if you don't believe these levels are possible, you're right. I'm a firm believer in this concept: whatever you believe is true, is true to you, regardless of the facts. The servant leader operates from such a powerful position of opportunity that they look at problems from a core thought of reconciliation (core thought at Level 5). In as much, servant leaders become bridge builders. Conflict becomes an opportunity to reconcile differences and grow as people, teams, and organizations.

Make no mistake: Everybody Wins doesn't mean the servant leader gives in to the whims and wants of those they lead, nor do they ignore challenges. It's simply not possible. What Everybody Wins *does* mean is that a servant leader has the belief that what is *best* for all can be found if sought...and they relentlessly pursue it.

Levels 6 and 7 start getting into more esoteric territory. These are the levels of mystics and religious leaders. And while many of us get glimpses of 6 and 7, very few people spend a lot of extended time there, although I believe we get to experience levels 6 and 7 more often when we become more conscious.

A FEW ADDITIONAL NOTES ON THE ELI

- At any given time in any given day, you could experience a mix of all of these levels. We are at a higher consciousness when things are going well for us and tend towards lower levels when things are not going well for us.
- Level 1 is not inherently bad as Level 7 is not inherently good. There are times when people are actually victimized. There are times we should be legitimately angry. Let's not live there, however. Conversely, total nonjudgment (Level 7) is not always useful. As leaders, we have to use our subjective reasoning a lot and we need to be able to judge appropriately.
- Those who choose service-oriented professions like helpers, healers, clergy, and healthcare tend to run in the mid-Level 3 to Level 4.
- The most successful and highly rated leaders in the world tend to operate at a Level 5 consistently.
- I am not an ELI/IPEC Certified Coach, but they do exist, and I highly encourage anyone intrigued by this info to find one of those coaches and take the assessment.

Since this tool has been around for a couple of decades, there is data around the average score. The most recent data suggests the average person's anabolic score is 3.25. Just think about that for a second. Think about the people you work with, the people you work for, your team, your direct reports, and your co-workers. On average, they are essentially coping at work on their very best day. Does this resonate with your experience?

What's interesting is, recent research around employee engagement seems to support this kind of data in a sense. According to Gallup, an average of only thirty percent of employees are engaged at work over the past eighteen years! (Gallup 2018)

Here's what's scary: Even though most workplaces operate at a 3.25, they talk a Level 5 game. Think about your company's mission statement and stated values and compare them to the ELI chart. Do most of them look like Level 4 and 5 or higher? Now think about the behavior and experience of the employees.

No wonder employees become disillusioned soon after hire. The lofty ideals that drew the candidate to the employer didn't match their actual experience.

What employees mostly experience are leaders and cultures who are operating and making decisions from a coping perspective but only on their best day. This means that the rest of the time, those leaders are showing up themselves in victim and conflict thinking. These employees and new hires are promised cooperation, service, creativity, wisdom, but what they feel is anger and apathy. And what's worse, the leaders have no idea how to change it and more than likely react to it with, you guessed it-conflict.

We've become accustomed to selling a Level 4 and 5 experience in our workplaces and delivering a Level 3 or below. We can do better.

The mission of this book, in many ways, is to help you shift what is more than likely a Level 1 - 3 consciousness to a Level 4 - 5 by adopting a servant leader mindset.

On the surface, it may seem Level 4 is sufficient. Level 4 sounds like servant leadership. But there is a major downside to Level 4 without transcendence to Level 5. Just like there are pros and cons to each of the aforementioned leadership styles, there are pros and cons to levels of Energy Leadership.

The downside of Level 4 is people take selfless giving to an extreme. They become so focused on fixing others in the world around them and end up frustrated when much of the time they cannot do so successfully. These folks have trouble letting go of what they can't control. This is what leads to eventual resentment and slipping back into an extreme conflict consciousness; they often give to their own detriment if left unchecked.

We aim for Level 4 - 5 because it incorporates service to others while taking care of self. This is a state of health in which everybody is better off including the leader. Everybody Wins.

Me and the ELI

When I took this assessment, I had just started in my new role as the Associate Director of a faith-based nonprofit. Much to my chagrin, when I received my results, I was astonished...and not in a good way.

You see, I've spent my entire life being an active member of my faith community. And since beginning my professional life back in 1995, I had spent a good fifteen years in faith-based environments.

As a result of exposure to this tool, I saw the core thoughts, feelings, and actions of highly effective leaders. Not only did I find these core thoughts, feelings, and actions admirable, but also, I found them to be in alignment with my faith (by the way, ELI is not a religious tool).

I don't believe you have to be a part of the faith community to understand these concepts, but this was my experience, and when I got my result I was greatly concerned. When I received my assessment debrief, I too received an anabolic (creative, constructive) and catabolic (destructive, tense) energy score. In other words, how I scored on my best day (anabolic) and how I scored on my worst day (catabolic).

My high score-my best day score-was a 3.2. Not bad and, at the time, slightly above average. At the time of my assessment, the average was 2.8.

But on my worst day, I was a 1.2. A *one point two*. And what's worse, through the subsequent coaching, it was revealed that I felt that 1.2 about seventy-five percent of the time. This did not line up with who I wanted to be, who I even thought I was, and it certainly did not align with my faith. You see, the anabolic and catabolic energy level scores are important but what was more important was how often I experienced those energy levels.

So, my question to you is, based on this brief overview of the ELI, where are you? Would your employees agree? How are you feeling most of the time? Take a look at the chart again and get honest. I would like you to think very critically about how you're feeling when you go to work every day. Are your days filled with compassion and peace or are they filled with apathy and anger?

Are you generally able to accept the things that happen around you and access wisdom and creativity from time to time? Or are you cooperating only because you don't want to lose your job and you're just marking time until retirement?

Please know, it is very common to be unaware of the core thoughts in that first column. While thoughts create feelings and feelings influence our actions, this concept doesn't mean we are *aware* in that order.

Sometimes you're more aware in your feelings. You may notice first if you're feeling peaceful or angry all the time. Or maybe you've noticed some of your actions on the chart or in my descriptions. Trace them back to the core thought or Level.

I noticed my feelings. I realized often that I felt angry and apathetic. This new information caused me to recognize some of the conflict and victim thinking that was going on in my mind. It also gave me huge clues into why I was getting certain results and how it directly related to my actions. Knowing and understanding how far I was from where I wanted to be was a painful realization.

I hope you develop a better understanding of where you are today, not to feel shame but so you can take the step of charting a path to change.

This new awareness helped me chart my path and it's the path I share with you in this book. Developing an understanding of servant leadership behaviors is only about twenty percent of becoming a servant leader. The remaining eighty percent of servant leadership is about mindset, and I believe if you can work on your mindset, that twenty percent behavior piece will fall into place more effortlessly.

Here's a recap of some ways you can informally evaluate where your leadership is today compared to servant leadership:

- Evaluate broad examples of Traditional Leadership vs. Servant Leadership
- Assess against list of leadership styles
- Become more aware of one's own 'energy leadership' and how often you find yourself in Level 1 and 2 vs. Levels 3-5

4
PROCESS: BRIDGE THE GAP TO CHANGE

Prior to my first coaching experience, I had no idea how to change the way I experienced my life. I had heard all the societal memes related to living in the present, creating my destiny and leaving the past behind; I agreed with them and yet, none of them were actually operating in my life. My tendency was to "Amen" these ideas while remaining personally unchanged and therefore in self-deception. You could say my attraction to the ideals of 'living your best life' were aspirational not functional. This habit caused much confusion and frustration for me because I saw those ideals as attainable, just not for me.

But once I learned I could change my life by changing how I perceive my life, I became unstoppable. I finally realized that my aspirational life was within reach. The growth that ensued-and continues to this day-positively improved my work performance, my personal and professional relationships, and helped me finally gain control over my seemingly incessant anxiety.

So far, you have learned a bit about servant leadership, other leadership styles, and the ways leaders can show up in their "Energy Leadership". Hopefully this has created a gap for you in that you see a more desirable place to operate from; a place that may seem far off right now.

It is not.

But like any new awareness, awareness alone is insufficient unless you understand how to use it to bring about the change you desire. Without a path and methodology for change, you won't change. In fact, awareness without the tools to change can increase your pain. Being more aware of not only the need for change, but also the possibility that your life and the way you experience it can be better-fantastic even-and then not having the tools can be very frustrating.

First, rather than simply giving the five servant leader mindsets, I want to show you how to make small shifts toward embodying those new mindsets, slowly and effectively. To accomplish this shift, I want you to understand the general process of change I used that created such a huge shift for me. Then, you can apply the concepts in this chapter repetitively to each of the ideas in the following chapters. This creates an opportunity for you to both practice the tools of change, and to do so while learning the five key mindsets.

And the best part about these tools is you can apply them to your whole life, not just work. In fact, I've often said, the best leadership development fundamentally and positively changes you as a person. This process can and will do exactly that if embraced.

YOU ARE NOT YOUR LIFE

In order to consider this model for change, you'll need to consciously separate yourself from a few things. The first is that you are not your life. You are not the events of your life. You are not the pain or the joy of your life.

There is you and then there is what has happened to you. Your worth, your value as a person, is not tied to your circumstances.

This is my non-negotiable for you: You are one hundred percent worthy, one hundred percent lovable, one hundred percent capable. Your life and circumstances have no bearing on these truths. If you were abused, if someone said you weren't enough; even if you messed up. You are worthy *by default*. Nothing you have done or will ever do will change this. No accomplishment or failure changes this default.

Starting from a place of worthiness is what gives you authority over your life. It's the first step to recognizing you are the author of everything *after* an event.

YOU ARE NOT YOUR THOUGHTS

Now, this concept may be disconcerting for some. The idea that you are separate from your thoughts may be new and even hard to believe. Or maybe you've simply never considered this idea at all. Many of us believe we are the same as our thoughts, meaning we have a thought and since the thought is there, we believe what it tells us and never consider the thought is separate from us. Your thoughts are just narratives in your brain. Think of them as letters and words on paper. That's all they are-like an LED screen across your brain.

Just because words that form complete sentences run across your brain doesn't mean they are true and doesn't mean they are inherently you. They are neutral. They are powerless. They just exist.

Take a moment right now and pause. What thoughts are you having right now? Write a couple of them down, no matter what they are. No need to write a paragraph, just the first few thoughts that come to mind.

See? You just observed your own thinking. You are not your thoughts. You *have* thoughts.

If you are not your thoughts, then where do they come from?

Your thoughts *come from you* but are not necessarily rooted in fact or truth. Your thoughts are based on how you perceive the world around you, influenced by messages you've received your entire life through experiences. Most of your thoughts are automatic and occur primarily in the subconscious and immediately create an emotional response. You can bring your thoughts to the conscious by slowing down and intentionally thinking about your thoughts, yes. But no one can do this every waking hour. Thus, the vast majority of your thoughts remain unconscious.

Everything, from how you were raised to what you've been taught, influences your automatic thoughts. If, as a child, you were told that you were worthless and couldn't do anything right, you may have a lot of automatic thoughts in agreement with those beliefs. If you were parented in a way that was supportive and encouraging, more of your automatic thoughts may be in alignment with those positive ideas. I mention childhood influences only to help you understand where some of your automatic programming comes from, not to assume any type of acumen in healing the past.

Take a moment and think of the most recent disappointment or failure you experienced. How did you react in your thinking? While these are extreme examples, which statement below fits best when you think about your reaction?

- I can't do anything right.
- Why do bad things always happen to me?
- I'm sad about this set back but I'm going to try again.
- Failure is just a stepping-stone to success!

If your typical reaction is closer to the first two, you may not realize there are those who react more like the second two. If you cannot fathom that quick of a bounce-back, your programmed thoughts are on the negative, self-defeating side. What's interesting is, no matter the reaction, the situation didn't change. The only thing that changed was the thought *about the situation*.

YOU ARE NOT YOUR FEELINGS

Just like your thoughts, you are not your feelings. You feel feelings but they are not you. You can feel sadness but that doesn't mean you have to be a sad person. Do you see how easily we internalize feelings and make them the same as our person? This is not a denial of feelings. This is a powerful acknowledgement of feelings.

When you can separate yourself from your feelings, you can observe them for what they are, trace them back to thoughts, and use them for their true purpose-signaling.

Because here's the thing: positive thoughts create positive feelings and negative thoughts create negative feelings but not all negative feelings are damaging. I'm not interested in denying or necessarily changing your negative feelings. What I'm interested in helping you detect are *damaging feelings*. If you are sad that a loved one died, that sadness feels negative or bad. But it's not damaging. Being sad when someone dies is normal and healthy. Life is both good and bad; positive and negative. It is quite normal to experience both.

I believe we humans have a tendency to over-identify with our feelings to the point they become damaging. For example, anger turning to resentment. Being angry can feel like a negative feeling, and it is. It is also a normal response to many different types of stimuli. But because I got angry at something doesn't mean I have to overidentify with that feeling and move into feelings of *resentment*.

This is why it's so important to understand the difference between you and your feelings. Without this separation, you cannot observe your feelings and evaluate them. Without this evaluation, the feelings are mismanaged and misinterpreted by being attached to your value as a person. For example, "I am unworthy" vs "I am a person having unworthy feelings". The first is a statement about the value of a person, the second is not.

Because of this separation, you can now accept you are *having* certain feelings (no need to deny them) but *you are not those feelings*. Your feelings are not you, but they are a part of you.

THE GOOD NEWS

First, you cannot change what has happened to you, but you don't have to remain the victim in your own story. Right now, you can look at your history and see yourself as the victim or the champion. You choose! Are you stuck in reliving abuse from the past or the overcoming young professional who achieved their dreams in spite of their abuse? You get to write that story today.

I'm not suggesting you pretend you didn't have negative experiences, rather, that you choose how you see yourself today as a result of those experiences. You literally get to choose. And that's the part of your past you can change today.

Second, you can choose your thoughts. You may not have control over that first thought or meaning you give to a situation or event; you do have control over what happens next. You can challenge that thought and choose a new one, a new thought that creates the life you want.

Finally, you can choose your feelings. Your feelings come from thoughts, pure and simple. If you feel awkward at a party, it is not the party making you feel awkward, it is your thoughts about the party. We all tell ourselves stories all the time and those stories (thoughts) dictate how we feel. Want to feel differently at that party? Change your thoughts.

THE NEED FOR CHANGE

Everyone experiences pain in life, but pain can turn to suffering if left unchecked. Please know I fully expect all of us to have a good mix of both positive and negative emotion in our life; a mix of joy and sadness. It would be ridiculous and downright irresponsible for me to try to convince you that through your thinking you won't have to experience negative feelings. We all have good and bad feelings or feelings that we associate as both negative and positive.

But when that pain turns to suffering, more often than not, it is self-induced through our thoughts and feelings. I

53

want to help you identify where you are causing your own suffering and how you can make different choices about your thoughts and feelings so that you can get your joy-to-pain ratio back in balance.

You remember my story, right? I was in conflict seventy-five percent of the time. That meant nearly four out of five days at work, I was miserable. After this revelation, I soon learned a process showing me how I was the cause of the most acute suffering in my life. I discovered I actually had control over how I perceived the events of my life, my role in those events, and the associated feelings. What's more, I found those feelings largely dictated my actions which gave me my results. I used to think that my feelings were caused by my results, but the exact opposite was true.

The process I learned is nothing new; however, my hope is to give you my spin on this method-a spin that made it simple and accessible.

If you could figure out a way to rid yourself of unnecessary suffering, would you give it a try? I hope so.

THE PROCESS OF CHANGE

After understanding the difference between me and the rest of my life, including my thoughts and feelings, I came to realize that much of the way I experienced my life was a result of my thinking. This is where the process began.

I had to think about my thinking. I learned about limiting thoughts. As you can imagine, limiting thoughts are any thoughts that-you guessed it-limit you. They are derived in part, from what psychologists call cognitive distortions. David Burns, author of *Feeling Good: The New Mood Therapy*, popularized cognitive distortions by creating common names for them. (Burns 1992)

Instead of covering all fifteen cognitive distortions, I've chosen four broad categories of limited thinking plaguing the workplace and our lives on a regular basis. I base this on repeated conversations with clients in the grips of these limited thoughts.

- **Extreme thoughts**: these kinds of thoughts are if-then, this or that, black and white, always-never thoughts. Limitations in science and math are useful but in life and in your thinking they are not. Extreme thinking tells us there are only one or two options. Have you ever heard of being stuck between a rock and a hard place? This is extreme thinking and it is limiting because it gives you an excuse to not create multiple options to a situation.
    - **Solution**: Whenever you're stuck in extreme thinking, just stop. Force yourself to think of more than two options. There are always many options. Even if the options you think of aren't appealing to you, think of them. This will get you into creative mode and out of this place of stagnation and victim thinking.

- **Untrue thoughts:** You may not realize it, but many of your thoughts are simply untrue. They are really your opinions that need to be challenged. When Karen didn't say "Hi" to you, was it really because she was aloof and dismissive? How can you be one hundred percent sure your opinion of her behavior is her actual motivation? You can't be sure unless, of course, you ask. You believe it; however, because her behavior reminds you of something in your past, your programming told you Karen was dismissive.
    - **Solution**: Ask yourself if what you're thinking can really be proven as fact with firsthand knowledge. Are you projecting your opinion onto someone's behavior and accepting that opinion as truth? If so, reframe. If your untrue thought was the worst, what's the *best* thought you could have about the situation that you can believe? Think on that, instead, since you can't know the truth of it right now. You might as well

believe something good!

- **Victim thoughts**: These might be the worst. These are the thoughts that keep you racing for someone to blame while ignoring your responsibility in a matter. But victim thoughts show up in more subtle ways. For example, when you run out of gas on your way to an appointment, would you have the tendency to say, "Ugh! This always happens to me! I can't ever get my shit together!" That's a victim thought. It's also untrue, more than likely. "Always" is an extreme thought and that's also not true. Every time you get in your car, you do not run out of gas (if you do, your car may need repair). But that second part, about getting your shit together, that's a cop-out. You have the ability to see that fuel indicator and make choices about when you are going to get gas. A victim doesn't take responsibility for their part in the pain being experienced. Note: Taking responsibility does *not* mean blaming or shaming yourself.
  - **Solution**: The quickest way out is to ask, *what's my part in this situation?* and take action.

- **Conflict thoughts**: Conflict thoughts are when we simply want things and people to be different. This can be a blatant conflict thought expressed through actions and aggressions on our part or a simple refusal to accept a situation as it is. We can literally demand people be and do different things. But more often than not, we just wish. We want the world and the people in it to show up in ways that don't frustrate us. We live in constant mental conflict with others because we cannot accept things as they are.
  - **Solution**: Every time you have a thought that you want someone to act or be different, just know, it's your unwillingness to accept something as it is. Instead, choose new

thoughts that support a new attitude of acceptance. My favorite is to remind myself that just like me, everyone else gets to choose how they show up.

The limiting thoughts I had usually created damaging feelings. Damaging feelings come from a particular set of limited thoughts that attack our value or identity in some way.

Damaging feelings tend to result in unproductive habits. Unproductive habits are the things we do that create our results we often say we want to avoid.

How do you know if you have unproductive habits? Look at your results. Is there something you keep doing but you don't know how to stop? Unproductive habit. Just telling you to do something different isn't enough. If it was, wouldn't all of our unproductive habits end? For change to occur, you must reverse engineer the process that created the unproductive habit.

It all starts with your thoughts.

My goal is to help you better identify your limiting thoughts so you can start to choose new ones. But here's the bottom line: moving away from limiting thoughts and towards liberating thoughts is good for you and gives you better results. When thinking about how limiting thoughts begin and the path they take, I like to describe them as a hula hoop.

At the top of the hoop is an event or circumstance. Then, as you move in a clockwise direction, that Event creates a Thought. The Thought you have is largely informed by the meaning you give to the event, usually based in past experiences. That Thought creates the Feeling; the Feeling inspires the Action and your Action gives you your Results. I call it a hula hoop because the process is cyclic. I find it helpful to remember that you are in the middle of this hula hoop and everything swirling around that hula hoop is your responsibility. It's easier in print, however, to view it like a circle or a Hula Hoop, as in Figure 7.

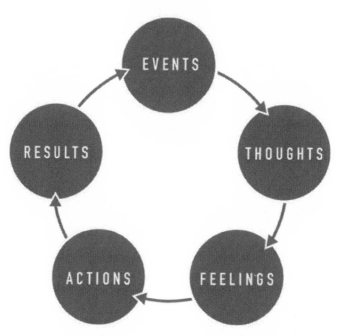

Figure 7

So how do we arrest these limiting automatic thoughts? The first step is awareness. We begin noticing our thoughts. For some people, awareness occurs first in their thoughts but for others, awareness shows up later in the Hula Hoop process. For example, I know I'm having a limiting thought when I feel anxiety. Anxiety is actually a physical response and I feel anxiety in the top of my belly. So, for me, awareness starts in my feelings making a physical manifestation. For others, awareness happens at the Action stage. In other words, you begin to notice you keep behaving a certain way and don't understand why you keep up that behavior. For example, you notice you lose your temper and yell at your kids or significant other when they leave dishes in the sink. The thought about the situation and the feeling of anger totally bypasses your awareness. All you notice is a pattern of yelling when certain things happen that you do not like.

Or maybe you are simply noticing some results in your life that are not what you want. The victim would blame outside forces but no more of that for you. Suboptimal results can usually be improved by taking responsibility for our part in creating them. But first, we have to notice them and admit they aren't what we want.

Stop and think for a moment when you have your most noticeable, visceral reactions. Are you experiencing a physical sensation? A strong feeling? How about a verbal outburst (action)? Maybe you notice a pattern of losing relationships (results). Pay attention to those repetitive patterns. They are speaking to you!

Which of the following processes sounds more appealing?

Limiting Thoughts–Damaging Feelings–Unproductive Habits

Liberating Thoughts–Desirable Feelings–Productive Habits

Since this is the first time working through what I will call the process of developing a servant leader mindset via my Identify-Challenge-Change method, I'll describe what I mean by each of the three steps and then provide a specific scenario to progress through each of the steps.

IDENTIFY

Once you get better at noticing the patterns you can start asking some important questions to help you identify where you are in the Hula Hoop. In other words, where in the Hula Hoop did you notice something was off? In your thoughts, feelings, actions or results? Here are some questions to then work through:

- What's behind this feeling? Why am I feeling this way?
- Where did that thought come from?
- Why do I keep behaving in a way I am not proud of, that I don't like?

What are the thoughts I'm having?

Wherever you are becoming aware in your Hula Hoop, that's where you start asking questions of yourself. The goal is to answer the questions as honestly as possible, really searching yourself for answers, whatever those answers are and without censor. There is no shame or guilt involved here. Think of yourself as a scientist, observing a subject *curiously*. A reputable scientist would not bash the subject for being what the subject is. No! The scientist would observe and ask questions for the purpose of learning and discovery.

Once you have identified the place in your awareness that is damaging to you, try to trace it back to the core thought. Just because the Hula Hoop model moves from Event to Thought to Feeling etc. doesn't mean you are aware of your limited thinking in your thoughts first. You may be aware that you are having a damaging feeling first; or, you may notice you behave in an unproductive way habitually. Regardless of where the need for change occurs to you, use the Hula Hoop process to get the root of the problem: your thinking.

So, if you realize you're experiencing undesirable results, first ask questions about your own actions. What got you here? What did you do? What part did you play? Then, how were you feeling when you engaged in those actions? Were you angry, fearful, sad or lonely? What were the feelings? Then, what thoughts were behind those feelings? Get to the core, root thought. This is the thought you will challenge.

THE SCENARIO: Brian is the Controller at his company, and he is currently training a new billing specialist, Aaron. Despite Aaron's transferable skills and expertise, Aaron is not picking up on his job responsibilities quickly enough for Brian. Brian repeatedly asks Aaron for updates on progress and Aaron is usually late or nonresponsive. Brian is angry and sends an email to Aaron that Brian quickly regrets. Brian has done this before but this time he's working with a coach and brings it up in his coaching session. At this point, Brian believes his problem is outside of himself. His problem is Aaron's lack of performance. He believes his frustration would be lessened if Aaron would simply 'do his job'. At the same time, Brian is not happy with his own action of sending a volatile email once again. Brian's coach asks Brian what he was feeling at the time of writing and sending the email. Brian quickly named the feeling: anger. Working backwards in the Hula Hoop, Brian's coach then asked Brian what thoughts he was having that created the angry feelings.

This is where Brian got stuck. Brian did not believe that his thoughts created the angry feeling; rather, the behavior of Aaron. Learning this new paradigm, Brian's coach was able to help Brian discover the thoughts that created the angry feelings. And not just the initial thoughts but the deeper fears behind those thoughts.

At the end of their session, Brian came to realize the thoughts he was having was that he, Brian, would be seen as a failure if Aaron didn't perform. Brian wasn't actually angry at Aaron...he was afraid of failure.

CHALLENGE

Once you've gotten to the root thinking behind your issue, you can challenge that thinking. You can easily use one of these four methods to challenge your thoughts. Start with the first and move down the list if need be. Most of our thoughts never pass the first challenge test, but in case they do, move to number two and so on. Notice: you are not challenging an event (i.e. Something a person did or what they said), rather, you are challenging *the root thought you are having about the event*.

1. **Truth**: Is this thought *really* true? Can I prove it is fact? Am I just assuming something but don't actually have firsthand knowledge of this thought being true?
2. **Extremes**: Am I having an extreme thought? Am I seeing something as black and white, right or

wrong, this or that?

3. **Responsibility**: Have I played a role in this situation, even if it's very small? What part did I play in the negative outcomes? Am I playing a victim? Do I see myself as a helpless target? Am I throwing up my hands and giving up?

4. **Choices**: Am I ignoring other choices just because I don't like them? Am I defaulting to having no choice?

Getting good at asking and answering these challenge questions will retrain your brain to think differently over time. And yes, I know it seems this takes too much time, but with practice, it will become more and more automatic.

THE SCENARIO: Now that Brian understood his core thought: "I am going to fail", he could challenge it. First, Brian challenged this thought with Truth. Is it really true that Aaron's failure is Brian's failure? Not really. What else could be true? How about this: Aaron is responsible for Aaron's results and Brian is responsible for Brian's results.

Is Brian's thought extreme? Yes. Being overly responsible for another person's performance is an extreme (yet very common) thought.

What about responsibility? What responsibility does Brian have in the situation? Brian realized maybe he wasn't doing all he could to understand what Aaron needed to succeed and was leading from afar.

Finally, Brian challenged his thinking with assessing his choices in the matter. Brian began to see that just because he felt angry, he didn't have to act on it. He also realized he had choices around what Aaron's performance really means. Aaron's lack of performance didn't have to mean Brian's failure as a manager.

CHANGE

The final step is to make a new choice-a choice in alignment with the results you want in work and life. Here's a follow up question for each challenge question to bring you to *change*.

1. **Truth**: What do I actually know firsthand about this situation?
2. **Extremes**: What are some less polarized thoughts?
3. **Responsibility**: What role do I want to play in this situation? How do I want to show up, regardless of how others show up?
4. **Choices**: What are all the other choices I can consider as options?

Another quick challenge for those of you who really struggle with damaging feelings:
- What am I feeling?
- How do I *want* to feel?
- What thought would create that desired feeling?

And then choose. Your brain cannot think two thoughts at once. You have to think on purpose!

THE SCENARIO: Brian made a few key choices. First, he decided to take note every time he felt this kind of anger and to not act on it until he assessed the root thought behind it. Second, Brian sought help from his supervisor on how to better lead Aaron. He realized he wasn't doing his part in training Aaron effectively. And finally, Brian decided to stop sending angry emails...period.

RESISTANCE

You've probably heard the Carl Jung quote, "What you resist, persists" (Seltzer 2016) and I agree. However, I want you to be aware of what you're resisting. I encourage you to make note of any and all resistance that bubbles up as you continue learning this new process-write down the resistance if you have to. What might "resistance" look or sound like?

- This is bullshit.
- This will never work.
- I've tried that before and it didn't work for me.
- I'll never change.
- This is too hard.
- This is too easy.

Every time you have any sort of reaction, that's resistance. A drug reaction is usually one that comes on fast and has negative consequences. A drug response is gradual and has positive or expected consequences. In like manner, focus on when you *react* to a new idea-it's sudden and typically negative.

The act of writing down your resistance will help you get in the practice of identifying thoughts you're having that you may or may not have been fully aware of previously. No need to elaborate-short sentences or phrases are fine, as long as you remember or know the context.

Resistant thoughts are to blame for our inability to change. When we know something is good for us or have a desired future state and simply cannot get there, I am willing to bet there's a resistant thought lingering in the unconscious backdrop of our thinking. This is why I want you to make note-I need you to be more aware of what you resist.

What follows next are my five core mindsets of servant leaders. For each of these mindsets, I will define the mindset, give examples and support and then ask you to take yourself through Identify-Challenge-Change for each.

You cannot embrace these new mindsets unless you first uncover how you unknowingly already resist them. By the end of this book you will have gained experience in challenging and changing your own thinking, while at the same time retraining your brain to more fully embrace the mindset of a servant leader. You ready?

FIVE MINDSETS OF SERVANT LEADERS

5
MINDSET ONE
VULNERABILITY: GIVING AWAY POWER

WHAT IS VULNERABILITY?

Whenever I work with a team of people and ask them what comes to mind when I say, "vulnerability," many of the responses are either negative or related to "oversharing". Those adverse responses are magnified if there are any current or former military in the audience. Some military folks I've met in my workshops relate vulnerability to weakness and, moreover, something to be exploited in an opponent. So, when I suggest vulnerability as the first (and arguably primary) mindset of the servant leader, there is considerable pushback.

The dictionary definition of vulnerability is "the quality or state of being exposed to the possibility of being attacked or harmed either physically or emotionally" (Lexico 2019). Well, no wonder there's so much resistance to this idea, especially from a leadership perspective. Generally speaking, we humans try to avoid harmful situations, both physically and emotionally. And leaders are human, so it makes sense we engage in the same avoidance at work.

Despite the definition, I keep coming back to the idea of vulnerability as a mindset. I see beyond the definition and recognize vulnerability as sort of a path; maybe a required path to reach certain destinations or results. In other words, vulnerability might be risky and feel uncomfortable (maybe even dangerous), but it seems to be necessary to creating the kind of connection we all seek and yet find so elusive. Then, when I reflect on the twenty attributes of servant leadership, the following seem to require vulnerability from the leader: honesty, integrity, trust, appreciation of others, empowerment, visibility, listening, and delegation. With these many attributes involving vulnerability, I simply could not ignore its importance.

UNDERSTANDING VULNERABILITY

Vulnerability has to do with bringing our most real and true self to everything we do. It takes vulnerability to step into the 'A' of being a R.E.A.L. leader: Authentic. Being authentic and being an authentic servant leader, however, are not necessarily the same thing. I could argue that if simply being authentic is enough, I could be authentically unkind and meet the criteria! But since my desire was to show up like a servant leader, I had to figure out, not just how to be *more authentic*, but how to be a servant leader *authentically*. I was and am not interested in faking my way to servant leadership; I want to embody this stuff.

This is why I stress mindset first. This is why I spent so much time defining servant leadership and providing what I hope was a desirable image of who a great leader is. My hope is this kind of leader becomes the type of leader you want to be, one step at a time. By authentic, I'm referring to who you want to be and how you can authentically represent who you want to be. This is not a "fake it til you make it" strategy but rather an awareness that who you are authentically today may not align with servant leadership attributes.

Vulnerability is not only important because it helps us

get clear on our desired authentic self, but also important because it requires us to work towards meaningful connection. In other words, the way we connect with people has to be purposeful and significant. Oftentimes, we find it easy to be vulnerable with people that we like, know, and trust but find it more difficult to be vulnerable with people that we loathe. The servant leader exercises the mindset of vulnerability with all. It is important to note that vulnerability is not the same as disclosure. Dr. Brené Brown, a research professor at the University of Houston and renowned author, speaks of this distinction on her televised special, explaining that vulnerability is less about disclosure and more about the quality of what is disclosed. (Barbara Markway 2019)

The importance of vulnerability cannot be overstressed here. If your desire is to grow in a servant leader mindset, learning to authentically servant lead through meaningful connection will require a mindset of vulnerability.

BARRIERS TO VULNERABILITY

While vulnerability may connotate weakness, there are other connotations that may stop us from embracing this idea. For example, vulnerability can bring up feelings of uncertainty. Dr. Brené Brown draws key connections between the risk and uncertainty involved in vulnerability (Brené Brown 2012), so this concern is not unfounded. For many of us, uncertainty in any kind of relationship leads to a lack of trust and therefore a lack of disclosure ergo…a lack of vulnerability. So, for this and other reasons, we get out of practicing vulnerability. If not uncertainty, maybe vulnerability means "blind trust" to some. To be clear: vulnerability is not indiscriminate disclosure and blind trust; it is not literal weakness or straight up uncertainty. It is, however, uncomfortable and, my dear friends, there is no way around this discomfort.

DISCOMFORT AND FEAR

So how do we get away with a lack of vulnerability? Dr. Brown infers we essentially run from it by engaging in controlling behaviors designed to create predictable outcomes. (Brené Brown Ph.D. 2017) But here's the problem: all the most delicious, memorable, and truly visceral experiences aren't planned and controlled. They happen many times, in moments of "emotional exposure" and it is this type of exposure that creates opportunities for love and belonging…yes, even at work.

It might be strange to think about love and belonging when you think about work, but knowing how much time each of us spends in the workplace and how much many of us really want to be a part of something bigger than ourselves, love and belonging make a lot of sense. Wouldn't it be wonderful if we could find more belonging and feel more attached to something bigger than ourselves at work where we spend so much of our time? Vulnerability is where it all starts.

Brené Brown mentions "emotional exposure" in her work and even includes it in part of her definition of vulnerability. Leaders do not typically fear for their lives physically, meaning, they don't fear physical exposure; but those who struggle with vulnerability more than likely fear emotional exposure. One of the biggest ways a leader can share power is to operate with a degree of emotional exposure. Emotional exposure can take many forms for a leader. Admitting when you're wrong, asking a direct report to teach you something or even saying, "I don't know" are all forms of emotional exposure.

This kind of emotional exposure creates the vulnerability to share power and sharing power is a servant leader move. The leader who cannot empower his or her direct reports because of fear they will mess up…they have a vulnerability issue. The manager who chooses to never ask for input has a vulnerability issue. The sales executive who refuses to distribute leads has a vulnerability issue.

In each scenario, the leader is driven by some

underlying fear of exposure. Maybe the fear is that the direct report will fail at completing the project and make the leader look bad. Maybe that manager never asks for input because he unknowingly believes a leader should be seen as having all the answers. And that sales executive? That person more than likely fears that the salesperson can't close the deal.

So why would a leader even consider embracing a mindset of vulnerability if, by definition, that vulnerability creates the potential for harm, uncertainty, or fear?

I'm not suggesting indiscriminate vulnerability. Vulnerability requires a degree of trust and trust sits on a continuum. I am more vulnerable with my husband than someone I've just met. My choice to be more vulnerable with some more than others is rooted in discernment and experience. You can learn when and how much to give when it comes to vulnerability-at home and at work.

The natural ability to build trust and therefore, utilize vulnerability, is influenced by many factors. Your personality, how you were raised, and your experiences definitely play huge roles.

I'm naturally trusting, to a fault. If trust is on the left side of the scale and skepticism on the right, I'm a hard left. And while I believe this is a great way to show up in the world, there are drawbacks. For example, I have to ask good questions and dig for details when working on contracts. Otherwise, I miss really important specifics and may ignorantly sign on the dotted line. This personality trait of mine signaled to me that I need to do a better job of putting agreements, plans, and ideas in writing and ask the same of those who work for me. That way, when there are conflicts, we have a record of our agreements to one another. This may sound like an obvious step to some but for me, totally unnatural. In fact, to this day, when I have a consultant sign a Statement of Work for myself or my organization, I still feel like I'm telling them I don't trust them. It's just how I'm wired. My trusting nature has resulted in offering up too much vulnerability too soon and sometimes to the wrong people. I've been hurt and had too many lessons to count in this department! Working on my vulnerability mindset means I need to be a little more self-protective because it's better for all involved.

On the opposite end is someone who is extremely skeptical. This person will typically err on the side of giving no trust and expecting trust to be earned all the time. (This is the person I need reviewing my contracts!) A more skeptical person or leader may tend to micromanage, see the glass half empty, and (sometimes unknowingly) emotionally abuse people.

While these examples on the continuum of trust are helpful, I want to further explain levels of vulnerability so you can assess where you are and then see there is a sensible path away from unhealthy vulnerability towards appropriate vulnerability.

Sightless Vulnerability

The most extreme version of vulnerability is what I call Sightless. A person with Sightless Vulnerability is someone who rarely, if ever, discerns who to trust and how much. This person has little to no discrimination and what's worse, is largely unaware they show up in this manner. Sometimes called "over sharers," this person blindly trusts those they meet and hire, often resulting in disaster, citing they simply "make decisions from their gut". A leader with this quality may freely delegate and because they are so trusting, they actually abdicate in that they are completely out of the loop. This leadership style is perfect for those who are autonomous performers but terrible for a newbie who needs a lot more direction. In personal relationships, the Sightless can take an extreme form, including the attempt to continue pleasing those who bring harm.

Passive Non-vulnerability

People who operate with Passive Non-vulnerability typically protect themselves through withdrawal from others. Unlike Sightless, who can't see that his or her environment is unsafe, Passive readily sees the lack of safety and hides. To the extreme, Passives avoid hurt and rejection by withholding any and all trust and vulnerability in an effort to control their world. At work, Passives are those who avoid conflict, having the tough conversations, and taking appropriate action. These folks don't want to "upset the applecart" so they remain silent.

Aggressive Non-vulnerability

On the surface, Aggressive Non-vulnerability looks like Passive because both are motivated by a desire to avoid something that doesn't feel secure. The difference is in the approach. Aggressive Non-vulnerable individuals actually move towards people and use their own social abilities, intellect, and negative emotions to control others. This is a more active approach that creates the distance the Aggressive Non-vulnerable needs to continue in order to feel safe and avoid vulnerability.

Perceptive Vulnerability

While there is still risk of hurt involved with Perceptive Vulnerability, this person understands the importance of boundaries and has learned to draw them in a way that allows for relationships to grow without opening up oneself to extreme harm. This person is in essence saying they will be vulnerable to the level that they perceive the other person is worthy of their vulnerability. (Springle 1994)

Needless to say, I highly recommend Perceptive Vulnerability. With this approach, the vulnerability to exhibit is in line with the relationship and works to protect all parties involved. While there is no guarantee you will never be hurt, you can use the idea of Perceptive Vulnerability to better evaluate when, where and to what extent you are vulnerable with others.

WHY IS VULNERABILITY IMPORTANT?

Developing a mindset of vulnerability not only creates an awareness and openness to one's own weaknesses, but also develops the readiness to share those weaknesses with others.

Traditional leaders exploit the weakness of others for their own selfish devices. This exploitation may come in the form of subtle manipulation all the way to overt corruption and mistreatment. The servant leader, however, leverages their own weaknesses as pathways for coaching others, making vulnerability safe for everyone.

The candidness necessary for such behavior makes weakness okay. For far too long, workplaces are places where we have to get it right, all the while sitting in a role we're not suited for. What about acknowledging what we aren't good at so that we can identify who is? Without vulnerability, leaders won't find this out about their people, and they need to make this practice commonplace by first exhibiting it themselves.

PRACTICE

There are ways you can begin to practice adopting a vulnerable mindset. The first way is simply knowing and expressing your actual wants and needs versus what you think people think you want. I believe this is a simple truth, but not an easy one. This requires you to actually know what you want! You may have to think about your wants in certain situations. Then, this approach requires you to have the courage to say what you mean and to do so in a kind, effective way.

Knowing what you want and expressing it keeps you out of the controlling zone. So often when I refrain from sharing my truest self, it is because I'm afraid of your reaction or wanting to avoid your reaction to my truest self. All my life I withheld what I really wanted and needed in the name of being nice and accommodating. But underneath, it's rather aggressive because it's an act of control. I want to control the environment and your reaction to it, so I don't have to deal with the fallout. As a result, my needs continue to go unmet and my resentment grows. By the way, I was definitely an Aggressive Non-vulnerable.

Take time to know what you want, how you really feel

about a thing, and then only respond honestly. If you can't respond honestly with kindness, decline to respond. I do this all the time.

The second way to practice vulnerability now is to ask for help. One of the biggest ways you can show vulnerability and share power with those you lead is admitting that you need help and that you don't know everything. Have you ever been in a conversation with a boss, where they asked a question and you pretended to know the answer? Especially when you knew you didn't know it? How about as a leader? Undoubtedly, there have been many times you've been put on the spot. Is the temptation high to have an answer right away, every time, even if you don't actually know the answer?

Being a good leader does not mean having all the answers, although this is a common hidden mindset. If you have to pretend that you know all the answers, there is no way that you can show up as vulnerable which undermines your potential to create significant, meaningful, and purposeful relationships.

Let's stop. Instead, let's say, "I need to get back to you on that-I want to be sure to get you an accurate answer." This response indicates you don't know it all, yes, but it also communicates that you care enough about the relationship to get them the best answer. Or better yet, what if we practiced saying, "I don't know but I'm willing to find out or find someone who does!"

The third way you can practice vulnerability starting today is by listening to others without judgment. It can be hard to do this. I'll be honest; every time someone's talking, I'm immediately thinking of how I can fix their problem and what's wrong with what they're saying. Instead, if I can listen with curiosity, I get out of judgment and find the opportunity to engage by asking meaningful follow up questions.

People can tell if you're listening to respond and usually do not want you to solve all their problems. I heard it said, to give advice is to others is an intrusion. To give advice to self is growth. When I listen without thinking of what advice I can give, I can listen with curiosity.

IDENTIFY

Earlier in this book, I said you would have a chance to practice the model for change every single time you were introduced to a new servant leadership mindset. "Identify" is about stirring up any resistance you have to a new idea or approach. This is how we bring old thought patterns into your awareness.

Now that we've covered what I mean by vulnerability, why it's important, and some ways you can practice vulnerability, let's *identify* some ways you may still resist this idea.

- What gets in your way of being more vulnerable?
- What are some reasons you believe vulnerability is a bad or useless idea?
- Have you come to the realization that your efforts to be "nice" are actually manipulation?
- Do you reject the idea that vulnerability should be based on trust and that trust is a process?
- Maybe you're afraid people will take advantage of you.

I want you to get really specific and pause right now, take time to write down all the ways you think being vulnerable is simply not going to work. Go ahead and do that now.

CHALLENGE

Bringing up resistance is important because it lets us know what our true thinking is. Our true thinking is what creates our feelings; those feelings inform our actions and our actions give us our results.

Remember the quote, "What you resist persists"? This is why I can't just leave you with a new awareness of your resistance. Being aware of how you resist a new idea is only the first step. It persists because the old way of thinking isn't challenged. So, let's challenge. Choose the strongest reaction that you had to vulnerability. Look back at the resistance you identified above and choose the one that feels the most visceral to you right now. The key is, we are not challenging what happened or the concept itself (whichever applies), but rather, we are challenging *what we think about the new concept* or what we think about what happened. Reminder: We challenge for Truth, Extremes, Responsibility, and Choices.

Truth
- Is it really true?
- How do I know?
- What proof do I have? (And your proof has to be firsthand knowledge, not assumptions, not insinuations or judgments.)

Extremes
- Is this "black or white" thinking?
- Am I caught between two extremes?
- Are any of my pushbacks "this or that" statements?

Responsibility
- What role have I played in the situation?
- What responsibility do I have in this area?
- Am I keeping a story alive and thereby revictimizing myself?

Choices
- What choices do I have in this situation?
- Am I getting stuck between a rock and a hard place? If so, what are at least three other choices I have?

CHANGE

The final step is to choose a new truth. The old truth was your resistance or pushback to vulnerability. That old truth was challenged and hopefully you have identified some choices that give you some new ways to view vulnerability. What new truth will you embrace? Hint: pick the one that brings you the most positive emotion possible, the one that is in alignment with what you *want* to experience, regardless of your reality at this moment. You create your future with these new truths.

Write down your new truth and every time you notice this pushback coming up inside of you, challenge it again with this new truth.

Let's take a look at a specific example of Identify, Challenge, and Change.

IDENTIFY
- "Vulnerability means I have to share my deepest secrets at work, and I am *not* doing that!"

CHALLENGE
- Is this true? Is it true all the time? What else could be true? Is this extreme? What's my responsibility and what choices do I have?
  - This is not true. What is true, is that I get to choose my level of vulnerability and I can base it on my perception of trust in a relationship. Also, vulnerability is not the same as disclosure. I can be vulnerable without disclosing personal information. It is my responsibility as a servant leader to begin to practice vulnerability because I care about myself and my people. I believe this is

good for me and others. I always have choices when it comes to how much vulnerability I exhibit. I can also test the waters of a relationship by practicing a little bit of trust and seeing how that goes. I don't have to pin myself into a corner.

CHANGE

- I choose to disclose meaningfully to those around me in ways that are in alignment with the level of trust I have with each person involved. I will choose one person to practice this within the next week.

I cannot overemphasize the importance of this simple (but not easy) process. I too thought it was overly simplistic, but I quickly found the discipline of it was quite the challenge.

6
MINDSET TWO
SPIRITUALITY: CONNECTING TO A HIGHER PURPOSE

WHAT IS SPIRITUALITY?

I believe connecting meaningfully to a higher purpose involves a spiritual awareness of sorts. In my experience, the term "spirituality" generates mixed responses. Even a short Google search of the word 'spirituality' brings up a multitude of resources ranging from mainline Christianity to palm readers. Some people are weirded out by the term spirituality for fear it refers to religion. Or others may shy away because it suggests something New Age (in some religious circles, this is a no-no). But the term spirituality doesn't have to be religious or creepy.

I worked through several other ideas for this chapter in an attempt to avoid this somewhat troublesome term; however, I could not get away from the connection I see between servant leadership and spirituality. Due to the wide range of understandings about spirituality, I want to simplify what I am and am not referring to. I don't provide this explanation to create an official definition but rather to give a servant leader context for the word as used in this book. And like the rest of this book, this is not meant to carry some sort of scientific efficacy but rather what I have experienced and believe to be true regarding the topic of the servant leader mindset.

WHAT SPIRITUALITY IS NOT

Spirituality is not religion; however, I understand and respect the connection. I'm not suggesting the servant leader must embrace religion of any kind to embrace spirituality. While many people find spirituality in religion, I do not believe religion to be inherently spiritual. In fact, based on my current understanding, I would not describe most of my early religious experiences as spiritual at all. Emotional at times, yes. But not spiritual. This also means the servant leader can very well embrace religion and possess spirituality too. One does not equal the other and they are also not mutually exclusive.

Furthermore, I do not believe the servant leader must embrace a belief in a deity to be spiritual. This is often a way to organize and even institutionalize faith and spirituality, but it is not in and of itself spirituality. I do believe there are tremendous universal truths found in many religions, but religion does not own those universal truths; they have simply found a way to conceptualize them into a practice and/or tradition. This is not fundamentally good or bad, it just is.

WHAT IS SPIRITUALITY FOR THE SERVANT LEADER?

When I refer to spirituality, I am referring to two things: the parts of your life that are distinguished from your physical experience and macro idea that you are connected to something bigger than yourself.

Everything you cannot see, hear, taste, smell, or touch but know to be real is spiritual-especially that which you perceive and do not perceive that transcends your thinking but also impacts your thinking. The importance of starting here is that the servant leader acknowledges this realm influences our physical experience even if we do not or cannot fully understand it. Spirituality is the exploration of what can't be seen but only experienced from a place that is somewhat hard to explain. I'm talking about your interests, your opinions, your approach to life, and what drives you. *The "you" that makes you...you.* You have a body, but your body is not the sum total of what makes you, you. Your body helps you experience you! Spirituality is the place from which you frame situations in your world that have the potential to create or destroy meaning in your life.

The servant leader is connected to this spiritual part of themselves and the world around them. They are connected and aware of their own drives and motivations, their desires, and their approach. Additionally, they understand these factors are also at play for others and are at play in the world, all of the time. The servant leader understands that interests, opinions, approaches, and drives determine how people show up in life, impact how they interact with others, and influence how decisions are made. Even if people aren't completely aware of them all of the time, these unseen aspects of our lives exist. Because so many choices are unconscious, the servant leader commits to an effort to intentionally align with this leadership style. To create this alignment, a spiritual connection is required-a commitment to looking at the unseen.

Someone who embraces a spiritual mindset is embarking on the work of uncovering what guides their choices, attitudes, and decisions. Another way to think about these guides is to call them beliefs. Beliefs are just thoughts we think over and over again that are perceived as truth and that which are largely unconscious. Someone with a spiritual brings these beliefs to the conscious level so as to challenge them and believe differently if a previously held belief is not beneficial, or worse, is discovered to be harmful. This is done so as to bring alignment between who we are and who we want to be.

Not everyone is aware or even desirous of knowing what motivates and influences their thinking; they may not even care that a greater spiritual awareness can positively impact these very same aspects of their lives. Can these individuals servant lead? In my opinion, they can. But, until they experience a more transcendent awareness of these unseen facets of the human experience and their impact on leadership, the fulfillment promised by servant leadership is limited.

WHY IS SPIRITUALITY IMPORTANT?

Having a spiritual mindset is integral to connecting first to yourself and then others, to a higher purpose. The servant leader sees a connection between this unseen world in their own life, links it to the seen parts, and sees how all of it is connected to something bigger than themselves. Because the servant leader sees this approach as vital to finding their own meaning at work and in life, they creatively help others find this connection as well. The servant leader is connected to a higher purpose and can creatively help others do the same. The recognition that a higher purpose is available and actually helps people achieve more fulfillment in life optimizes the servant leaders experience and ultimately the experience of those who work for the servant leader.

Connecting to a higher purpose helps all of us find more meaning in work and life. In fact, this connection can greatly improve our engagement in life and work even if we are not passionate about everything in our life and work. Why? Because purpose is uniting, and passion is just about you. Purpose involves all of us! In Dan and Chip Heath's book, *The Power of Moments: Why Certain Experiences Have Extraordinary Impact,* they explain this concept in a simple way. They describe passion as isolating because it is hyper-focused on the individual. If something is *my* passion, it is mine; it is not yours. However, purpose is something that a group of people can feasibly share.

This does not mean passion is not important but rather, passion on its own is limited.

If you are like many others, you have been told to just follow your passion if you want to be happy. Oftentimes, this conversation is directed at what we choose to do for work. It makes sense on the surface, being told to follow what you love and are most excited about, to go find a job that allows you to do what you are passionate about every day.

In *The Power of Moments*, the authors refer to a study comparing purpose and passion. This study came out of University of California Berkeley's Professor Morten Hansen. His survey included 5,000 employees and then connected those survey results with employer performance scores. However, this study revealed some very surprising information about the connection between performance, purpose, and passion.

If you ask employers what they want, many will say they want people who are excited about what they do. This passion and excitement are sometimes seen as a means to get more done because people will work harder at something the love. Or will they?

Professor Morten's study found that people without purpose or passion are very low performers-bottom tenth percentile. This is no surprise. He also found that those with high passion and high purpose were outstanding performers-eightieth percentile. No headline with this finding. Note: there are a lucky few in this category!

What he found that surprised leaders is that purpose is far more important than passion. You'd think if someone had passion but little purpose, they would fare significantly better than those with low purpose and low passion. After all, if you're passionate about something, you will find purpose in it, right? Wrong. This simply was not true! If someone had passion but little purpose, they were only little better off than someone without either-twentieth percentile.

But get this, if someone had low passion but high purpose, they saw a major jump in performance: sixty-fourth percentile. This is such good news for employees everywhere because chances are, the majority of the folks working for you are not super passionate about their job-you may not be able to move the needle in this area for these folks. But you can help these people find a higher purpose in their work, and according to this study, this results in a performance improvement. (Heath 2017)

	High Purpose	Low Purpose
High Passion	80%	20%
Low Passion	65%	10%

Figure 8

However, it is difficult to connect others to a higher purpose if you are not connected to one first. And connecting to a higher purpose takes spiritual awareness. This spiritual awareness is what helps you make unseen connections to the bigger picture.

While the overarching purpose of this book is not to help you find your higher purpose, I do wish to bring some clarity around adopting a spiritual mindset. For me, a spiritual mindset has meant many things over the years, most of which were rooted in maintaining the appearance of being spiritual while feeling completely disconnected on the inside. But I'm thankful because this internal experience, this emptiness caused me to search for answers moving me beyond the typical "Why am I here?" in relationship to what I do for work. Understanding and developing a higher purpose is definitely important and the value of doing so should not be ignored. To that end, I'd like to present a basic exploration of understanding higher purpose and its importance for the servant leader developing a spiritual mindset.

INNER PURPOSE AND OUTER PURPOSE

If you are struggling to think about or figure out your own higher purpose, it may be because you have not tapped into your inner purpose first. When I say inner purpose, I'm simply encouraging you to look at certain things about you that make you, you. Your inner purpose doesn't have to do with what you do; on the contrary, your inner purpose is about what you are. This is where true purpose is found.

Even your attempts to define what you are can be done mistakenly in terms of the outer self. For example, I am a mom, a wife, an author, a person of faith, etc. The tendency is to answer *being* questions with *doing* answers because we can tie those activities to an outer purpose. *Doing answers* feel more concrete. *Doing answers* are much easier to identify.

The problem with this approach is your inner purpose is primary-it has to do with *being* only. Your inner purpose starts with the recognition of this fact: You are here. You exist. Do you know the chances of you existing? Dr. Ali Binazir, self-improvement author and "Happiness Engineer" did the math and found out that the odds of you existing are 1 in $10_{2,685,000}$. (Pope 2018)

That number is unfathomable! So, to start with "I exist" as the launchpad of your inner purpose is sort of challenging but I encourage you to just sit with the thought..." I exist".

To me then, your inner purpose becomes the 'getting to know' the you that exists. This is a gradual process of waking up, waking up to who and what you really are. The process of change introduced in this book about being aware of your thoughts and feelings serves the purpose of helping you to be more conscious of who and what you really are. And while I have attempted to share the information in a step-like process, the real truth is all you can do is be more aware. This, in and of itself, is your inner purpose. Just being more aware of your inner thoughts and who you really are, is enough to connect with your being, your inner purpose. Inner purpose is to be conscious, aware, to grow and change or even to awaken. This is our common inner purpose *and therefore shared by all.*

Your outer purpose, as previously stated, is related to what you *do*. Outer purpose can change over time and varies from person to person. The changing of your outer purpose is usually in connection to or correlation to the increased awareness of your inner purpose. The more aware you are of your being, the more intentional you can be about your doing. This awakening experience alone will impact changes in your perceived outer awareness.

It is my opinion that trying to figure out a singular outer purpose that is lifelong is a very limiting endeavor. The false belief that my outer purpose was some sort of lifelong calling actually created a type of identity crisis when my tenure in education ended. I had incorrectly connected my joy and worth in life with my outer purpose. This is something only an inner purpose can give. So, while your outer purpose may change, your inner purpose can give meaning, joy, and value to anything you do because it influences how you end up doing all things and why you do them.

As we wake up on the inside and become more aware of our inner purpose, there can be great alignment with the outer purpose. This alignment is a wonderful confluence of being and doing that are so connected, it is hard to tell the difference between the two. This isn't to say you can't do great things without this alignment, but without it, joy, fulfillment, and true enthusiasm for our everyday work will be lacking. Furthermore, this connection between inner and outer purpose brings meaning to even the mundane in life.

This is why spirituality is the mindset here. Becoming conscious of the inner purpose is a spiritual practice and process.

HIGHER PURPOSE-CATEGORIES

So then, your higher purpose is a combination of your inner and outer purpose. When this connection occurs on the conscious level, you will quite automatically see a connection to something bigger than you, at work and beyond.

Moving out from this somewhat esoteric idea of inner and outer purpose, there are some simple ways to look at higher purpose. To me, higher purpose usually falls into one of a few categories: Repairers, Tellers and Changers.

Repairers

Repairers are those that want to bring health, nourishment, peace, love, and concern to the world in one way or another. Often these people like to fix things that are broken in systems and people and/or prevent harm in those systems and people.

Tellers

Second, your higher purpose may fall into the 'Teller' category. Tellers are those who are usually gifted with wisdom and communication and they want to convey something that is important to them that they believe could be useful to others. Think of the person who potentially, like me, has learned a new process for thinking and thinks, "Hmm, this wisdom, this change that I've gone through, this message that I want to bring, might be helpful to others."

Changers

Finally, your higher purpose could be to be a 'Changer'. These are folks that want to innovate and bring big shifts. You'll see these people doing anything from sitting in pulpits, on the stage at political events, leading startups, making previous inventions and processes better and more efficient, all the way to marching to make a difference.

HIGHER PURPOSE-SEASONS

Your higher purpose is the big mission you want to achieve *at this time* in your life and your inner purpose is how that big mission gives expression in the world. In other words, your higher purpose can change based on the season of your life. Some of my mom friends have said they believe their higher purpose was related to motherhood until their children left the home. That parent-child relationship changed so drastically that the parent realized their role had changed...a new higher purpose emerged unrelated to raising children yet retaining the essence of that parent's inner and outer purpose. Your inner purpose can be expressed and benefit all things in your life, including your outer and higher purpose. With this in mind, the possibilities become absolutely limitless.

For example, there are lots of different people who write books like this who want to bring a message, but each and every one of us that create books have a totally different inner purpose. What our inner purpose brings to that big mission is vastly different from one another.

I remember when I first started thinking about writing a book years and years ago. I struggled so much with the idea that other people have already done it. As a result, I allowed that thinking to keep me from writing, until someone said something really important. They said, "Shannon, but *you* haven't done it." In other words, there isn't anyone who has the same inner purpose giving expression to an outer purpose quite like me...or like you.

Third, your higher purpose encompasses your whole life, not just what you do for a living. What you do for a living can be an expression of your higher purpose and when it is, your work will be more meaningful and fulfilling. But your work does not have to be a direct expression of your higher purpose. Maybe your everyday work makes your higher purpose possible.

Understanding the distinction between inner, outer, and higher purpose helps you to help others find and then connect their life and work to a higher purpose too and it all starts with a spiritual mindset. The connection simply begins with an awareness of the possibility of this connection. Then, you get to choose what the connection means.

HIGHER PURPOSE IN PRACTICAL TERMS

Finding your higher purpose and helping others do the same starts with a spiritual awareness and ultimately results in helping yourself and others align heads, hearts, and hands. Many leaders focus solely on heads and hands. Heads, having to do with what we know and hands, having to do with what we can accomplish. But what about the heart? The heart is where we find purpose.

EXAMPLE: Cathy worked for a transportation company writing code for the IT department. Her assignments were described in terms of what to do, with very little explanation on why. Cathy wasn't particularly jazzed about writing code, but her job paid well so she showed up and got the job done (heads and hands). She put in her eight hours a day with little to no complaining. As time marched on, Cathy became restless and started thinking maybe she needed a change of scenery, maybe she needed to work for a new company. Why? She wasn't sure, she just "wasn't fulfilled" so a geographical change might solve the problem.

Cathy began her job search and eventually landed a new programming job at a bigger company making $15,000 more than before. Surely, this would bring her the happiness she sought. But after the newness of the job and the challenge of learning new internal systems wore off, Cathy found herself in the same predicament: little meaning in her everyday work. Cathy was completely unaware of her motivations for even choosing the IT field, other than the pay was pretty good.

After a few years, Cathy got a new supervisor, Susan. Susan was a servant leader who truly valued people and was passionate about IT. Furthermore, Susan believed her purpose was to solve insurmountable problems. She derived energy from this purpose, and it drove her motivation to inspire others and serve other departments with IT solutions. In a way, you could say she was an "IT healer."

Susan noticed Cathy showed little excitement for her work and gave zero discretionary effort. Cathy's work was acceptable, but she wasn't a top performer. Susan decided to meet with Cathy and review her role and figure out why Cathy had such a lackluster attitude at work. Susan soon found out that Cathy viewed her work as only work; her job was simply to utilize her hands to give expression to what was in her head. So, as you can imagine, when Susan started asking heart questions, Cathy was a bit stunned.

Over a period of time, Susan asked Cathy about her education, wanted to know why she chose the IT profession. Susan learned what Cathy enjoyed most in life, what energized and drained her; she learned that Cathy was pumped about getting results, meaning, she loved doing something and seeing a result instantly. Cathy was a changer! Susan was then able to show Cathy all the ways her coding affected the efficiency of those who used the programs Cathy created. In time, Susan helped Cathy tie her head and her hands to her heart. Susan creatively drew a picture for Cathy, a picture of Cathy's higher purpose. Cathy eventually would say her higher purpose was to bring about significant, positive change for others, wherever possible. This was a purpose Cathy was able to apply to every area of her life, including herself, and in this she found tremendous meaning and fulfillment at her job, even though programming itself wasn't something she was passionate about.

Cathy needed a Susan. Cathy needed a servant leader who was connected to her own higher purpose and mindful enough to help Cathy connect to hers. Cathy found a way to connect her everyday life to something bigger than herself.

Your higher purpose need not be obvious to others, result in a big promotion, or create a national platform. But it does need to be bigger than you and your passions. I hope you take time to think about your life and what has influenced your life choices. I hope you become more aware on a spiritual level and develop an internal honesty about what has led you to where you are so that you can choose differently if need be. And from there, my hope is you discover your higher purpose too.

IDENTIFY

As you read through this section on Spirituality: Connecting to a Higher Purpose, think of any points of resistance. For example, do you reject the assumption that spirituality doesn't have to be religious? Or, are you having trouble believing that people who can tie their life and work to a higher purpose are better performers? Or maybe your resistance is that you are the one who struggles to connect your day-to-day life to a higher purpose. Maybe you simply can't find the meaning and believe it cannot be found.

CHALLENGE

Take a look at the ways you reject the ideas around spirituality and higher purpose. Challenge them.

Truth
- Is it really true?
- How do I know?
- What proof do I have? (And your proof has to be firsthand knowledge, not assumptions, not insinuations or judgments.)

Extremes
- Is this "black or white" thinking?
- Am I caught between two extremes?
- Are any of my pushbacks "this or that" statements?

Responsibility
- What role have I played in the situation?
- What responsibility do I have in this area?
- Am I keeping a story alive and thereby revictimizing myself?

Choices
- What choices do I have in this situation?
- Am I getting stuck between a rock and a hard place? If so, what are at least three other choices I have?

CHANGE

What new statements, thoughts, or beliefs can you craft that are better aligned with this servant leader mindset and in alignment with how you want to show up? Write a statement or two that represent what thoughts you will choose the next time your old resistance comes up.

7
MINDSET THREE
SURRENDER: LETTING GO OF CONTROL

WHAT IS SURRENDER?

The idea of surrender and letting go of control may seem counterintuitive for a book on leadership. If you're like me, you've been told that you control your destiny; that if you work your plan, your plan will work. These types of sayings and societal memes permeate our identity and can become the measuring stick of success. You end up believing, even if unintentionally, that these same concepts equate to your ability to control a situation. And, this control is linked to your results.

But how many times has your life unfolded exactly the way you wanted it? I'm serious. Think about every aspect of your life: work, family, friends, finances, health, and home to start. How much of this was truly under your control? Has your career, your job roles, the people who've worked for you, the people you've worked for, how many of these things have ever gone the way you hoped? Not much of my life has gone as expected.

Nonetheless, I found myself attaching to my results in

an unhealthy way. First, as a high school student. During this time in my life, I learned to plan backwards from a goal. And yes, I reached some of those goals, even if seemingly small in comparison to my present day.

Then, in college, as the stakes grew higher, I planned and planned some more. More success came...more proof to me that I had control over my destiny.

I believe planning, strategizing, and goal setting are important and positive behaviors if they are aligned with the right mindset. But for me, what began to develop was an attachment to outcomes giving me the illusion of control.

From as early as I can remember, I've been described as the proverbial control freak (although a recent assessment revealed, I don't really want to control anymore but I do enjoy being in charge). This control nature of mine kept me from enjoying life on many levels. My need for control took various forms; from healthy planning to unhealthy coping mechanisms, control marked my life. And looking back, I can more clearly see where this need to regulate all of my experiences served me well.

My whole family fell apart when I was in elementary school. Around fifth grade I noticed my mom was gone a lot only to later visit her in the mental health ward of a hospital. Later, my parents would divorce and with my mom struggling for appropriate care (mental health treatment was a lot different in the 1980's) while my dad figured out how to pay bills and run a business in her absence, us kids were lost in the shuffle.

During this same timeframe, I distinctly remember my parents taking me to a local park to play. By the time my sister was done playing and it was time to go home, I had just warmed up to the idea and was crushed that we had to leave. Two hours had passed. I was not ready to go to the park when everyone else was and I was just getting used to the park when it was time to leave. And while this is a simple, childish example, it stands out to me as an adult to this day.

So much of what happens to us as children is out of our control and we develop coping mechanisms to deal with each of these situations. Our coping mechanisms made sense at a young age but cause us pain as adults because their application is no longer working. And how do I know something is no longer working for me? Pain *in* my results. My entire world crumbled so no wonder I developed a keen sense for governing my surroundings. But like many childhood mechanisms, this control became maladaptive as I progressed into adulthood.

As an adult, this controlling nature made attempts to control things that cannot be controlled, like other people, places, and things. But I didn't know how to tell the difference for many, many years.

In my school leadership role, I attempted to control everything, from my task list to other people's perception of me-and only one of those things is actually within my control. Directing my tasks brought me career success but attempting to augment the perceptions of others? That created years of anxiety. So, life, circumstances, and other people have a way of challenging the need for control and either we learn and grow or remain in pain.

One of the primary places I, and probably many others, experience control issues or power struggles is in marriage. Marriage has a funny way of challenging a need for control and my marriage is no different. With my husband's permission, I now share our most challenging experience to date as a couple. While I have gradually learned to step by step let go of control over the course of my life, nothing propelled me to this mindset of surrender better than one of the most painful experiences of my life: watching my husband relapse in 2016.

Let me be clear: I did anything but surrender control when this happened initially. Oh, hell no. I checked up on him in every imaginable way. I tried to follow him when he left the house, I questioned his whereabouts when he came back home, and I demanded he stop "or else." This, my friends, is not the picture of surrender, rather, I was white knuckling this experience every moment of every day, unknowingly reducing the chances he or our marriage would recover.

My anxiety became insurmountable as I cried myself to sleep on a nightly basis. During the day, it was all I could do to smile and get through work appointments. There were many, many days I excused myself to the restroom just so that I could conduct breathing exercises to calm my stress and even cry. I prayed every prayer, meditated, sought professional help for myself, yelled at him and researched about the disease of addiction. I was truly at the end of my resources.

Once I reached the end of my capacity to solve this problem, I did something I had never done before. I found someone who also had this problem. You know what the first thing she told me to do? Stop trying. Stop asking, begging, checking messages, following, worrying, and even caring. She told me to surrender and let go.

What the…?

No seriously, this was my audible reaction. Who in their right mind lets go of a situation that *clearly* needs some direction? Am I right? And by the way, I am *super good* at giving direction to others so, you know, I can fix this!

When I looked up the word surrender in the dictionary, I found words like: "relinquish, to yield, to give up, to allow, to abandon or resign". These seemed to ring true, especially when I think of what the word surrender connotates. But a couple parts of the definitions really threw me off a little bit because they said this: "to allow, influence or to be influenced; to allow emotion." Whoa. I never thought of surrendering as *allowing* something. To me, surrender meant giving up, as in, like a total and complete wimp! But here's the thing-nothing else was working. Maybe, just maybe, there is a symbiotic relationship between letting go and allowing something to happen at the same time.

Herein lies what I have heard called a 'spiritual irony'. You know what you want, you might even have a good idea of the steps you need to take to get there and yet, surrender is asking you to let go of what you want. I wanted my husband to stop using drugs. I thought that was the single most superior solution to his problem (I admit, I also needed to work on my arrogance that I had the answer to his problem). It's very logical. Remove the drug use and I can go back to my happy-go-lucky life. What I had not learned was that the act of surrender often gets me what I want...and much more. But I had not yet learned this. To me, I got what I wanted through control. If it wasn't for the whole pesky "letting go" part, I could do this-All. Day. Long.

I must admit, however, I'm a slow learner when it comes to letting go of control. I didn't stop my destructive part of the situation for a solid sixteen months. I was steadfast in my pain, still believing that if he just loved me enough or if I could prove I loved him enough, he would stop. If he would just stop, I wouldn't be in pain. I still believed the cause of my pain was outside of myself. None of this is true, of course, I had to test it out! Eventually, I did let go.

Letting go meant I had to overcome the fears of letting go, or rather, what I associated with letting go. As I explored what letting go meant to me, I realized it meant things like, I was weak and didn't really love him. Or another way to put it...if I *really* loved him, I would hold on. So, the first thing I needed to let go of was my beliefs about letting go! This first step was crucial. In order to take hold of something new, I had to let go of something old. I had to be willing to be wrong.

The second step in letting go was to get my eyes off what I thought was the goal and onto myself. Specifically, I had to stop focusing on my desire for husband's sobriety and focus on what I needed for myself. I still knew my desired outcome (a sober husband), but I stopped trying to create it. I stopped taking the actions that were tied to my belief that I could create it. I stopped doing the things that weren't good for me, and then started doing the things that were. No more checking up on him, asking for updates on his whereabouts and demanding he quit what he was doing. Away with angry, empty threats (manipulation in disguise), and instead only spoke truth with kindness. Why? All of these actions decreased my anxiety and freed up my mind, body, and emotions for the good stuff. Good stuff like spending more time with friends, attending support groups, and reading books about my own self-care and personal development (instead of incessant hours on Google, researching ways to stop him).

Now, this is a book about leadership, and you may be wondering what in the hell this has to do with leadership. Please think in your mind about any work situation that is not at all what you want it to be. Or think of one from the past. Tap into your feelings of helplessness and rehearse in your mind all that you did or are doing now trying to control that situation to obtain your own preferred outcome. Make sure you choose a situation that, like mine, despite your best efforts has only gotten worse. I'm talking about the situation that makes you want to spit, yell, and quit all in the same sixty seconds. I'm talking about that boss who repeatedly displays an inability to lead, who makes empty promises, is "obviously" not qualified, and drives you up a wall. Think of the situation at work that deep down, you know you have no control of.

Yeah. *That* situation.

WHY IS SURRENDER IMPORTANT?

See, we all face circumstances in our lives that do not go according to plan resulting in an array of outcomes. Some of those outcomes range from mild inconvenience to complete and total disaster. On the positive side, those outcomes could also run the gamut of "according to plan" to unimaginable positive results! We rarely need help with the second kind. More than likely, we need a little more help with the undesirable side of these things.

Getting on the surrendered side of a situation gives you the space you need to act in alignment with a servant leader mindset as a whole. As long as you are in control mode, your thoughts and options are limited, thus limiting your results.

Once I finally got with the program of surrender, miracles occurred. About three months into my behavior change, my husband took notice. He would tell you that he realized I had let go, and that scared him. And I never once threatened to leave, divorce, or otherwise punish him through removing myself once I started my new surrendered approach. All my yelling, telling, pleading, and controlling didn't get his attention. My letting go did-*but this was not my motivation*. I didn't surrender and let go to get his attention. That's just another form of control. Any time you take action A in hopes of response B, that's manipulation. Instead, my letting go became about something very simple: *What do I need most right now in this situation that I have the power to give to myself?* This was in essence, surrender. I took control of the only thing I could actually control-me-and let go of what I could not-him.

The surrender created the space for him to see himself instead of me. The surrender gave space for him to see his part; he no longer could blame me for any negativity because I wasn't laying any down. He was left alone with his pain and his choices and that brought him face to face with himself.

Eventually, he went back into active recovery and has been sober ever since. Our marriage is more alive and vibrant than ever before. While I don't want to go through that ever again, I am so thankful for the lesson in surrender and what it brought to me, which was way more than I ever could have imagined. Please know, I am not saying that every time you surrender to a situation, your results will pop up petunias. No. This is not a guarantee. But I can promise, you will feel better and make better choices, which is always better for your outcomes.

My best efforts simply could not bring me what only surrendering control did. I wanted him sober-and yes, I got that. At no time did I imagine what his recovery choice brought to him as a person and to our relationship. I had no idea and I'm glad I stopped making my plans the only outcome I would accept.

See, when we don't like something that we can't control, we tend to commiserate with others who agree and then the group of us tend to come up with the best solution. Sound familiar for workplaces? All that energy spent on mentally controlling a situation that simply cannot be controlled. Control is an illusion.

CONTROL TAKES MANY FORMS

My lack of surrender and tendency to control all things has taken many forms. While not exhaustive, here are some big categories of control that have gotten me into trouble in the past.

Process

Much of human history is a story of process and progress. Many processes are man-made and meant to speed up progression. Take for instance travel. The desire to create quicker ways to accomplish the process of traveling gave way to the invention of flight. But what about processes best left to their natural arc, like personal growth? Can you control what you learn? Yes. Can you control whether or not you apply what you learn? Absolutely. But learning and application do not guarantee a specific, measurable personal growth that is the same for all. They are goals along the way of a lifelong journey-a journey unique to each individual. The same can be said about the growth of your employees. You can set goals and create objectives, but the ability to control the outcomes of said goals is an illusion. Don't be fooled-just because you applied X goals with Y objectives and you achieved Z outcomes with an employee, does not automatically mean your process will create the same results in another person every single time. Does this mean we do not set goals? Absolutely not. It does mean we recognize that our control is over the goals we set and the efforts we put into those goals. Our control is not over the results of those efforts. Controlling process in this instance is an attempt to get an employee to take the same path as another, expecting the same outcome. We tend to want and even expect others to develop and grow at our pace. But is this realistic? Whenever we engage in implementing a process involving others, we must let go of what happens as a result. We do our best to create the processes that are in alignment with our values, best practices, and industry standards but we must let go of the expectation of outcome. Then, whatever outcomes occur, new choices and maybe even the need for new goals emerge and we repeat the pattern. My former board president said this to me: "Shannon, work your goals and let go of the outcomes." Words I can live by!

People

You've heard it said you can't control others but the attempt to do so is common, although not in ways that may be obvious. I'm not talking about physical control, nothing easily observable. The attempt to control other people takes subtler forms in our day-to-day lives. For example, withholding information from a co-worker for fear of their response or as a passive attempt at punishment. This is a form of control because it is an attempt to control a response and/or prevent a certain outcome. This is also a form of manipulation. So, when someone says they withhold information so as not to hurt someone's feelings because they are trying to be nice, remember manipulation is not nice. What they are really saying is, "I don't want to be made uncomfortable by that person's response." It's truly a selfish act.

Have you ever done or said something out of the belief you could control what the other person thinks about you? "Well, I don't want them to think I'm _____." You don't have control over what people think, no matter what you do. It's also none of your business what they think about you. This attempt at control drains your energy and keeps your focus off what you can actually control: yourself. And bonus tip: people are allowed to think what they want about you, just as you are allowed to think what you want about other people.

Proving

I've tried to control by being overly responsible to prove my worth. I've taken on jobs and responsibilities of others just to be seen as the hero. If I could be seen as the hero, then I could ensure I was seen in a positive light. I was controlling others through proving myself. Proving caused me to lie a lot too. I would say 'yes' to things I really didn't want to do. That 'yes' was a lie and was motivated out of wanting someone to like me or prove my worth.

Preferences

I'm a firm believer in asking for what you want and not apologizing for your preferences. This is healthy. However, when you are in leadership, you will find a plethora of knowledge and expertise in considering the preferences of others. You are not betraying yourself as a person or as a leader when you let go of your preferences and consider and at times defer to someone else's, especially if it serves the greater good. Too many leaders get stuck in their own preferences and what makes them comfortable not realizing opportunities await in airing out the preferences of others. This takes the form of "my way or the highway" mentalities rampant in less-than-self-aware leaders who care more about their own comfort than the good of the team and organization. Important to note: I highly recommend verbalizing your preferences last. Open the floor up to everyone else's input and then express yours. As the leader, no one wants to disagree with you and once you bias your team with your preferred methods, solutions, and opinions, you take too big a risk for group think to set in and not enough of the best ideas to bubble up. But do express your preferences-just do so while considering others' first.

Past

This may seem strange, to consider controlling the past because after all, the past is over and cannot be controlled. I maintain we do our best to try anyway. We stay in the past by constantly wanting the present to be different. This is rooted deeply in a belief that if the past is rehearsed enough, we can prevent it from happening again or be more prepared if it does. This may work great for planning football plays and combat strategies but it's a destructive way to live our everyday lives. The only thing that can influence the future-as good if not better than imagined-is to surrender it today. Besides, our brains work hard to create a future in the direction of our strongest thoughts. If my thoughts are constantly in the past, in situations I regret, I'm going to more than likely keep recreating those situations in my future because my brain is so focused on them.

Predicting

Predicting is a coping mechanism we use to manage the discomfort we have with the unknown. This approach can be employed towards our own future state/plans as well as towards other people. I've done this in the most microscopic ways. Whether you are forecasting what a friend will say (and subsequently choosing your behavior and actions accordingly) to avoiding a tough conversation at work, assuming the conversation will go south, you're engaging in prediction. This is a form of living in the future and it is, in a sense, self-manipulation. There's a discomfort with not knowing what will happen so you may try to cope by predicting the outcome, falsely believing this will help you feel prepared. And unfortunately, your prediction is based on how you perceive the world and your past circumstances, which as you know by now, are not all based in fact.

Whenever you're predicting, you're staying out of the present and limiting your thinking to outcomes only. You're not considering all of the other possibilities that could happen if you approach the situation by letting go of what you can't control.

Peace

This may seem strange, but yes, chasing peace as an outcome can in some ways keep us from peace. We must know if our pursuit of peace is really an avoidance of something unpleasant. We can have peace *and* have problems. Peace is a wonderful pursuit, but not if it is motivated by running away from our problems. Peace is not the answer or the opposite of negative emotion and yet we treat it this way. In essence, we then strive for peace, but peace is not obtained by seeking, searching, and striving all the time. Peace is what we get when we feel the negative emotion and know it cannot hurt us. Peace is in the midst of the negative emotion. It's the "both-and," meaning, it is feeling the bad stuff and trusting it will be okay…to your very core.

The absence of peace is not the presence of negative emotion. *The absence of peace is the absence of surrender.*

SURRENDER, ACCEPTANCE, OPPORTUNITY

Acting from a place of surrender leads to acceptance which creates more opportunities, better outcomes, and more choices every single time. For example, when I am dealing with a difficult person, I may decide ahead of time how they are going to act in a particular situation. Then, I may predetermine my response or reaction. In doing so, I'm essentially narrowing my choices for how I want to show up based on an unknown future outcome. I've assumed how an interaction will go and showed up in a certain way as a result. I've already chosen behaviors that almost ensure a negative outcome, all because I couldn't surrender the future.

This process is inherently limiting. What I'm basically saying is, "I want to control how you act around me because I can't handle the discomfort of your reactions." Instead if we can simply accept that this person is a difficult person, this is who they are, we can then make the choice that *is* within our control: how we want to act, what we want to say, and how we want to say it; and those answers are based on who we want to be. What person do we want to be in that moment? We can now choose from an array. We have all kinds of choices available to us now because we can choose to be any kind of person we want. We can choose whatever attitude we want; we can choose whatever words we want. Tons of choices open up. However, when we make a choice based on the *other* person, we are now automatically limiting our outcomes based on something that we simply cannot predict. Acting from a place of acceptance and surrender is where you find choices.

WHAT PREVENTS SURRENDER?

So why don't we do this? If there are such wonderful, freeing benefits to surrender, why not just...surrender?

Fear. There are a lot of core fears associated with surrendering. We're afraid of what will happen if we surrender. We long for certainty and having an assured outcome. This is normal. And while I bet this is easy to agree to, what happens when we unknowingly get caught up in that fear?

For example, what if we say what needs to be said in that staff meeting, say it in a way that's in alignment with our values even though we know it might be a hard thing to say and a hard thing for others to hear? We're so afraid of how others will respond. We're afraid of the outcome and that we won't be able to predict and control them.

Not only are we afraid of what will happen by letting go, we are afraid we won't get what we want. If we are honest, there's an underlying belief that by controlling and manipulating, we can get what we want in a situation. When one of my daughters decided she didn't want to continue in college, I had a choice to make: impose my advice and direction (without being asked) for fear that I won't get what I want, or, deal with my own discomfort of letting her figure out her own path. What do I want? I want each of my children to earn a college degree. It's important to me. But I actually do not have control over this. Any advice or guidance would simply be a way for me to resolve my own fear and lessen my discomfort. Yes, I could convince myself and others that my actions are motivated from a place of love and a desire to see my children succeed. But who says a college degree always equals success? There's proof this isn't always true! Who says the lack of a college degree equals a lack of success? I also cannot prove this is true all of the time.

Really what this is about is me imposing my beliefs

about college education onto my daughter. Why? I cannot let go of her decision. I cannot surrender my need to impose my ideal life onto her. The real truth is, I have no idea where her life will go and neither does she. She could change her mind next week or next year. She could never get her degree. By letting go and surrendering my need to control, I leave space for her to explore options without needing to also push against my will. And for me, this comes down to my general faith that things work out. They have for me, and trust me, I've made many terrible decisions. If I believe God is able to make sense out of my choices, do I also believe He can do the same for her? Yes, I do.

In thinking and researching this part of the book, I came across an interesting quote by Einstein. He said, "The most important decision we make is whether we believe we live in a friendly or hostile universe."

Getting what I want and trying to control the outcome so that I get what I want might come from a core belief that I live in a hostile universe. It's a fear that if I don't control things and make sure they turn out the way that I want, I'm not going to get what I want. Or, the thought that I need to choose my actions based on the way I want you to react to my actions; otherwise, I'm not going to get what I want from you either. This fear of not getting what I want may be rooted in the belief that the world is out to get me.

But is the world out to get me? I have plenty of proof in my life that it is. I did not have an ideal childhood. In fact, my adolescent years were riddled with a terribly broken home, absent parents, abuse and more. But still, I get to choose what I believe. I choose to believe I live in a friendly universe, and no matter what happens, things are going to work out for me. That "even without my input" things can work out for me...even if I don't try to control them. Why? Because the universe is friendly, and it's conspiring for my best interest. Does this mean I expect *all* things to work out positively for me? No. Does this mean I believe only good things happen to me? No. But this perspective does assume that in the whole of my life, overall, things are and will continue to work out for *my best interest*. I chose this perspective because this perspective created the experience *I want to have* in my life, not the experience I already had in my childhood.

So, what are some practical ways we can practice surrender in our work and in our life?

You are not a big deal

Many, many years ago when I worked at the school, I had the opportunity to go on a senior trip as a chaperone. On this senior trip, we went to Andros Island, Bahamas. Andros Island is maybe a few steps ahead of a third-world country. It is highly undeveloped. As you drive down the streets, you see homes in various states of completeness.

From what I understand, there is not a lot of credit available on that island, at least not at the time when I visited. You could tell because there were homes being built that had a foundation and weeds grown up everywhere. And then another one would have a foundation and maybe the first floor built but no siding or insulation, just wood. And, again, weeds everywhere. There were, of course, finished homes as well. Due to the lack of credit availability, homeowners had to wait to save up cash for each phase of the building process and the time in between could be months or even years. There were also those who still lived in settlements, consisting of people who build their own hut-like homes and grouped them together in the middle of the woods.

What stood out the most about Andros Island was the beauty of the beaches and the water. Of course, Andros is set in the Caribbean-the view is amazing! Our accommodations were at the Forfar Field Station, a field study program of International Field Studies (IFS). We each stayed in huts. These huts were not insulated. They had no air conditioning. They had some warm running water, but you couldn't flush anything down the toilet that wasn't liquid. I'll let you go ahead and just think about what that means.

I'll admit, the first couple of days that we arrived, I had a hard time with the living conditions, especially when they recommended sleeping under a mosquito net. Not necessarily for the mosquitoes at night, but because of the spiders that were as big as your hand.

The discomfort of my hut gave way to something I experienced that has stayed with me all these years. The staff of Forfar showed us an enormous sand bar, just off the coast, in front of our row of huts. It was close enough that if the tide was coming in, you would have plenty of time to get back to shore. And far enough away that when you stood on the sand bar, it felt just a little bit like you were standing in the middle of the ocean. It was the coolest thing.

I'll never forget how I felt in that moment because I'd never felt it before in my life up until that time. I realized how insignificant I am.

Faith plays a huge role in my life, and I believe there is intelligent design at work in the universe. I call that God. I believe that I'm important to that creative force-I believe we all are. At the very same time, the irony of insignificance set in. This isn't meant to invalidate anyone's emotions or how things are going in your life, any pain, abuse, trauma, or misfortune. I just think it's good to remind ourselves that we aren't that big of a deal. We are not more important than anyone else. And sometimes, what we want and what we're trying to control is really just us on a little sand bar out in the middle of the ocean trying to pretend like we're the king of the world when really, we're just a little spec on this big blue planet.

Let go of personal preference

The second thing you can do to begin to surrender control is to let go of your personal preferences. As soon as you make a personal preference your choice, you've now limited yourself and said no to all of the other choices. I understand there are things in life that force you to make a choice. When you're hiring someone, you need to make a choice. When you're picking a marketing partner, you need to make a choice. If you're designing a new logo and there need to be colors that need to be chosen, you have to make a choice. It's good to remember your preferences are just yours-it doesn't mean they are the best. It can be helpful to be cognizant of where your preferences really don't matter. They are not the right way. They are just *a* way.

Meditate

Another way you can begin to surrender and let go of control is to meditate. Now, don't worry, if you're not someone who meditates, you don't have to start with sitting in silence with a gong in the background for twenty, thirty, or sixty minutes. One of the ways you can bring everyday meditation into your life is by simply noticing. Notice what's around you right now.

Become conscious of your surroundings and name them in your head (or out loud if that works better). When you're driving in your car, notice the trees you're passing. Notice what the highway looks like. Are there flowers on the bushes? Is it raining? What's the weather like today? Notice if you have a pain in your ankle or if you have a little headache; anything you can physically see or touch keeps you in the present moment. Your mind has a superpower: it can time travel to the past and future. But your body and your surroundings are ever-present. Noticing them is all it takes to stay present too and presence is what meditation is all about.

This may seem like a very insignificant step, but I promise you it is powerful. Practicing this has helped me let go little by little and chip away at that control gene that is so hardwired into my being.

Categorize

Another way you can more intentionally work on surrendering control (work and life) is to get really strategic about what you can and can't control. Sometimes we just have to slow down and put things in their proper category. What can we control, what can we influence and what's left? Make lists if need be.

In most situations, there are parts you can absolutely control: Your words, tasks, efforts and planning. These are your action steps. They are things you can actually do. They are words you can say and choices you can make.

For example, if I'm working on a project with a co-worker and that co-worker is not pulling their weight, I cannot control that outcome. What can I control? I can have a conversation with them. I can express my expectations. I can ask them to leave the project. I can discuss it in a meeting with the two of us and our supervisor. When I identify what I can control, I'm identifying the things I have choices about. I'm identifying actions I can take. Keep in mind some of what you have control over may not be your favorite choice because you're afraid of an outcome. Leave those choices on the table; resist the urge to delete them. Keep them on the list for further consideration. Don't allow fear to determine what choice you make. Within the realm of the things you have control over, choose your actions based on who you want to be in each situation, not based on what you think someone's going to do or how they're going to respond. What most of us do in that situation at work is grumble over that co-worker's behavior and act like a victim. We never get clear on what we can and can't do about it and so we do nothing.

Then, look at what you have influence over. In that same exact situation, you may be able to influence that co-worker by having a heart-to-heart with them. Maybe you can ask them more in-depth questions around what's getting in their way of performing. Maybe you can influence the situation by offering to coach or advise them, taking a cooperative approach versus punitive. Maybe you're more experienced and more successful in a particular area, and they need a little help. You could potentially influence their performance, but you must always ask permission to intervene. When you simply take over, you do great damage to the other person's self-esteem and prolong the pain of having a co-worker who isn't getting things done. If ever you cross over into coercive, manipulative, or passive-aggressive behaviors, you are no longer working with your influence but relying on control. The ability to rightly divide what can be controlled and what can be influenced helps expand your choices. The more choices you have, the more empowered you feel.

And then finally, what's left. Whatever is left is not within your control, that's what you surrender. For example, you go to the co-worker, you realize you have control over asking them to get something done on time. You ask. They still don't do it on time. You accept they didn't get it done on time, but then that acceptance opens up another set of choices over which you may have control and influence over. Note: accepting an outcome does not equal approval. Acceptance is about *your* choice to deal in reality without languishing in what you wish would have happened instead.

The key is to continually challenge yourself around what you can and cannot control. Ask yourself: When do I tend to attempt to control the things I have no control over? When do I fail to take action on the things I do have control over? I suspect that as you commit to this practice, you'll find you have control over much more than you realized and will feel relieved at the letting go of all the other stuff you've been trying to control but can't.

IDENTIFY

Reminder: When you identify, you are bringing to your awareness the resistant thoughts you are having about a new idea. Resistant thoughts are clues into what you really believe and are what create your actual feelings and resultant actions.

What resistance do you have regarding the mindset of surrender? Here are some common ones:

- If I surrender, something bad will happen.
- I won't get what I want/need unless I'm in control.
- If I let go of control, my team will not meet their goal.
- If I engage the preferences of others, I'll be seen as weak.

CHALLENGE

Now, let's challenge one of the fears from above I commonly hear:

If I let go of control, my team will not meet their goals.

Truth
- Is this really true all of the time?
- What proof do I have?
- What else could be true?

Extremes
- Is this "black or white" thinking?
- Am I caught between two extremes?

Responsibility
- What is my role in goal setting?
- What is my team's role in goal setting?
- Have I operated in my role adequately?
- Have I held my team accountable to their roles?

Choices
- What choices do I have in holding my team accountable?
- Are there new strategies I could learn to let go of control?
- What can I learn about accountability and delegation?

CHANGE

How do you want to show up in this situation? The first step in establishing this new approach in change is to put first things first. A "first things first" is getting clear on what you can and cannot control. Second, for the things you have control over, identifying what choices you have. And finally, making a conscious choice.

Instead of trying to control others, take control of self. Oftentimes when we feel out of control, instead of controlling our own reactions, controlling our choices, and ceasing the manipulation and coercion, we try to control others. Controlling others can feel like the quicker win, but it isn't. Let's focus that control on the only thing we can control which is our self and our choices.

Not only can we focus internally on putting first things first, but also, we can use the language of inquiry. If we're feeling stuck between a rock and a hard place, like we don't have any choices, we can ask questions that open up lots of opportunities. Curiosity creates options. Believing we are stuck limits options. Asking questions may help us see things from another person's perspective that we had never seen before.

What choices do you have to control yourself when you must accept undesirable outcomes at work? If you don't have a team or even if you're at the top of your organization, many things are going to happen that are completely out of your control. What choices do you have at that point? How can you utilize positive language to gain more information about a situation to better understand it?

AN IMPORTANT NOTE ABOUT SURRENDER

Please know, your new mindset of surrender is not a veil for apathy and abdication. Apathy and abdication are rooted in Level 1 consciousness. The core thought behind the feeling of apathy and the action of abdication is victim thinking. So, while letting go may look (and at times feel) like giving up, the core thought is completely different.

8
MINDSET FOUR
DETACHMENT: DEVELOPING A NONREACTIVE PRESENCE

"The root of suffering is attachment." Buddha

WHAT DOES DETACHMENT MEAN?

Detachment as a concept has a basic single definition. The application of the idea of detachment can take on many forms and functions. At first glance, detachment has potential negative connotations such as being aloof, dispassionate, disinterested, indifferent, or even distanced. These synonyms do not seem congruent with servant leadership, much less quality human attributes. This is not what is meant by detachment in this book or in reference to servant leadership. Instead, I'd like to focus on alternate definitions of detachment and specifically how they pertain to establishing detachment as a positive servant leader mindset. Those definitions or synonyms include open-mindedness, neutrality, lack of prejudice or bias, fairness, and unselfishness.

Detachment isn't the removal of emotion or the denial thereof (as in the first set of synonyms like aloof or indifference) but rather taking responsibility for one's own emotions and not attaching them inappropriately to people, circumstances, and things.

When it comes to people, detachment may take the form of letting go of control, allowing people to make their own choices and truly deep down wanting them to do so; it may also include refraining from taking responsibility for someone else's emotional responses and even a pure commitment to never taking things personally.

Detaching from circumstances can include the ability to "stand outside" of situations and better evaluate them from a more objective point of view. It can also mean one does not allow events to dictate emotional responses such as being sad when we don't get our way but rather viewing the circumstance for what it is: we didn't get our way. In essence, detachment is about separating our biased meaning of a circumstance from the circumstance itself.

These few examples are in no way exhaustive but serve to show detachment in everyday life. But talking about detachment in this way simply does not bring much dissonance. Even if you struggle with detaching from other people's emotions, you probably agree it's a good idea to do so. You probably see the benefit of a work that would result in such detachment. Why then are we leaders so attached?

To better help me understand for myself, I evaluated my own life. Not from the perspective of what am I detached from or what should I detach from, but rather, what am I habitually attached to or what have I been habitually attached to in the past that ended up causing more pain than solutions for me? In my identification process, I found many ways I attach to people, places and things in unhealthy ways and a few patterns emerged along the way.

Work

One of the first and foremost things that I attached to was my work. Listen, I work hard. No one has to encourage me to work hard. No one has to remind me of due dates, deliverables, or deadlines. I. Am. On. It. I have worked hard to achieve personal and professional goals, salaries, bonuses, and titles (not bragging and there's nothing to be impressed with here-I'm not one hundred percent sure my goals were super lofty anyway). In an honest reflection of the achievement of past goals, I can share that at the end of them, I wasn't fulfilled and still felt quite empty. My attachment to work and achievement fell short in that they did not accomplish the fulfillment I believed they would. I'm all for setting goals, working with excellence, and achieving the things I set out to do, but my happiness and contentment was placed in the outcomes of those efforts and those outcomes did not deliver for me. Where did this leave me?

Well, I just need to set higher goals, make more money, achieve more dreams, right? If last year's achievements didn't create this undefined sense of contentment I was after, then I just need to push harder so I can reach that destination this year, right?

Wrong.

What I didn't know then that I am thankful to at least understand now is how much my worth as a human being was attached to my work. It's not like I had never learned the concept that *I am worthy as I am*. Every time I heard it, I agreed with it in my mind.

But my actions told a different story. My actions spoke of my true beliefs which included an attachment to this idea: work equals worth. When we attach our work to our worth, we make it a part of our identity. In other words, our work becomes who we are. However, I didn't figure this out from someone telling me like I'm telling you.

Maybe try this on for size. You know when you're attaching your worth to your work when the people who work for you fail or look like they will fail, and you feel angry and/or threatened *personally*. This is more than likely because failure at work feels like an attack on your identity. After all, work equals worth. So, when we become leaders and eventually must get our work done through the efforts of others, we then attach our own success to the performance of others. *If my team is successful, I am a success; if my team fails, I am a failure.* You may even react to those statements with something like, "But that's true!"

Here's why it isn't true. If your team is successful, you all *experienced a successful outcome.* If your team failed, you and your team *experienced a failure.* This is detaching from outcomes at work. It is not a denial of the facts. It is applying the truth of those facts to the appropriate place. But without this, we unknowingly place tons of extra pressure on others and ourselves out of an unconscious desire to protect our identity.

Let's not talk in extremes like failure or success. What about something more commonplace in everyday work, like basic poor performance of an employee? How do you react to poor performance? Does it anger you? Do you feel that your job, other people's perception of you, and/or your job security is at stake? If as a leader, poor performance creates these types of fearful reactions, I'd like to suggest to you that you learn to detach from someone else's poor performance. This doesn't mean you ignore and fail to deal with poor performance. Not at all. It means that someone else's poor performance has nothing to do with your worth as a person.

Now, is it possible you didn't lead them as well as you could? Maybe. But that does not mean their performance equals your worth. It simply means you have responsibility in leading your staff that maybe you didn't fulfill. You can learn and do better if you want. That's all. The elimination or reduction of personal emotion in this situation allows you to make more objective decisions about what is best for you and the poor performing employee. It can prevent you from lashing out and creating possible unnecessary punitive environments (formative correction always works better-ask a talented HR professional, I bet they agree!) Furthermore, this approach avoids the act of piling pain onto pain. There's the pain of not leading well, then the pain you add by making your failure to lead about your value as a person. It's just unnecessary to add this pain into the equation.

Detaching provides space to make different choices that have the potential to create better outcomes. For example, you might see a way to coach that poor performing employee, talk to them about taking on a different role, or maybe even have a calm conversation about transitioning them out of the organization. No matter which route you choose, the point is, when you are detached emotionally, you are able to choose what's in your own and your organization's best interest, as well as the best interest of the employee.

People

Leaders also get attached to people. Now, this may sound contradictory to the earlier chapter on vulnerability, which focused a lot on connecting meaningfully to people. But that is not what we're talking about here. We're not talking about disconnecting from the people around you. We're not talking about eliminating vulnerability because, remember, vulnerability is about how you want to show up. It's not about attaching to others in an unhealthy way.

We attach to people who work for us in an unhealthy way when we take on their emotional state, when we allow their drama to become ours. This is not meaningful connection at all. And taking on someone's emotional state as our own is not empathy either. Yes, empathy puts us in their shoes to be able to understand where they are coming from. But it is not meant for us to actually take on their emotional state which, in turn, can cause us to think less clearly.

I see this most often when I conduct initial meetings with employers, and they cannot move past all the petty, little arguments of their employees. They have a disease my kids used to have called the "yeah-buts" and the disease presents something like this:

Me: Let's identify some of your top line leadership issues. Is it okay if I ask you some questions?
Client: Yeah, but I'm wondering, how can I get the associates to stop complaining to me about overtime and all the bickering that goes on about time off? We have such a huge issue with them not aligning to our value of "doing whatever it takes." One time last week a manager…

Me: …patiently listens then redirects back to my question.

Leaders who are stuck in the weeds are over-identifying with the emotions and drama of their people. This is not sustainable and not an act of connection or care. I will go a step further and say it's more so a refusal to lead and take responsibility for their own part in creating the very situation they complain about. But I digress.

You can detach and genuinely care for people at the same time. I repeat: *You can detach and genuinely care for people at the same time*. With empathy, you can listen and even understand the difficulty they're experiencing without assuming their emotional state. This detached engagement allows you to empathize and remain a nonreactive presence so you can access the most objective ideas available to your brain, allowing you to see and deal with the situation in light of all the other components, rather than deal with the situation based solely on the other person's emotional state.

Early in my leadership career, about ten years after college, every teacher that walked into my office that was upset, made me upset. I thought I had to match their emotional tenor to *prove* I cared. But you know what that did? It got me all emotional and unable to make objective decisions. And I was miserable making decisions based on which personality showed up at my doorstep in the form of another teacher.

Detaching from people in this way accomplishes another really important task for leaders: your people learn to solve their own problems. Eventually I got sick of playing referee between teachers and students and parents. Finally, a teacher or parent came to me to complain about someone other than myself and I told them, "Go to the person you're upset with. I am not the go-between and the person you have a problem with is the person who can resolve this issue."

I only stepped in when either something egregious occurred (which was literally two instances in five years) or when the best efforts of others simply did not work. And even then, all parties had to be in the room with me; I then simply guided the conversation while those really involved actually solved the problem.

I couldn't do this when I was taking on all the emotions and drama of the people around me. Detachment is a gift I gave myself, as it allowed me to stop taking on the problems of others so they could solve their own problems.

When people at work solve their own problems instead of the leader rushing in to solve them, it allows others to learn, grow, and feel empowered. I've seen many leaders complain about employees, getting emotional about their performance or lack thereof. In their emotion, they rush to solve the problem by taking charge and solving the problem themselves. That employee's confidence is slightly diminished, and the cycle continues. The leader never addresses the core issue: their inability to lead an employee who is struggling. The leader hasn't learned to adjust their leadership based on the development level of the employee. This leads to frustration and mismatch between how the leader behaves and what the employee needs. And in those instances, the 'rushing in' is probably an inability to manage the discomfort created by letting go.

Instead, if the leader was able to detach from the problem, they could calmly and kindly hand the problem back to the employee, offer the appropriate level of direction and support while expecting the employee to solve their own problem. In this process, the leader is better positioned to evaluate what the needed levels of support and direction are. Furthermore, if the leader can then utilize skills of vulnerability, empathy, and understanding, they can still maintain and further a healthy connection, realizing that the employee can get the job done, resulting in a confidence boost for all.

Why do we remain attached to someone else's drama at work or elsewhere? Mainly, because we are unaware but also because we actually get something out of it. Being the hero, stepping into drama and saving the day can feel pretty good sometimes. That's the ego. This behavior is not sustainable and only serves to diminish everyone's ability to perform. Plus, you can't do this equitably across the board. Eventually, the most dramatic and time-consuming people take up eighty percent of your time while your nose-to-the-grindstone top performers get little leadership from you.

Another way I've seen unhealthy connection arise between employers and employees is when employers or bosses get overly angry and become embittered when people leave the organization. This is due to an unhealthy connection and a lack of understanding and acceptance that people come and go. People work for you for certain reasons and they quit for other reasons. Most of those reasons have nothing to do with you. And even if they do have something to do with you, that is simply the way it goes. A leader who can detach emotionally in this situation is a leader who can better enjoy their team in the here and now, without fearing loss. This leader accepts these losses are not personal and are a normal part of running an organization. The need to take it personally is a need to attach to the other person and their performance because after all, their performance is somehow tied to your success.

Need to Be Right

Finally, leaders could be served well if they detach from the need to be right. Remember this: If you are right, someone else has to be wrong…right? When we overly attach to our own beliefs, attitudes, and ideas of what is right, just, correct, and/or appropriate, we are essentially working against open-mindedness, which automatically creates an oppositional environment where we become unwilling to change, unwilling to grow, and unwilling to engage the ideas and input of others.

Is this the same as saying there are no right ways of doing things? Absolutely not. Take regulatory environments. I would imagine there are very specific processes and procedures that must be followed to ensure the safety of all. This is not what we're talking about. This is about detaching from the need to be right as a method for self-assuredness, especially in collaborative environments or times of ideation.

If you believe you are the smartest person in a room, then you believe your education, experiences, intellect, and decision-making abilities are superior to the collective wisdom of a group of people. Does that seem logical or even plausible? Does that sound humble and approachable? Does that sound like servant leadership? Not to me.

Leaders who need to be right and have the best ideas are usually ones who feel the lowest on the inside because without this public acknowledgement of their mental abilities, they have no identity. This results in the refusal to entertain other ideas, even ideas that would create financial health, employee safety, and align with best practices. I've sat in meetings where decisions were made against human resources standards for no other reason than the idea didn't come from the leader of the organization. The experience was the epitome of blind arrogance. No wonder these leaders have such high turnover-even if you could prove to them their need to be right creates a lack of morale, disengagement, and turnover, it wouldn't matter. Why? They didn't come up with that idea. Simply put.

Detach from being right. Let the good ideas bubble up. Everyone, including the leader, will elevate.

WHY IS DETACHMENT IMPORTANT?

Healthy detachment from work, from people, from our position, from outcomes, from being right, gives you the perspective to view a situation from a three-hundred-sixty-point-of-view. This is kind of like walking around circumstances as an objective observer. In this frame of mind, the leader is better able to see the problem for what it is, evaluate the varied solutions, and the impact of each considered solution. Once this is accomplished, the leader has a higher chance of making a decision that is best for themselves and best for the organization.

Detachment also gives the leader no room for playing the victim. Detachment actually empowers you as a leader because in this nonreactive state, there is no need to expend precious energy on placing blame; rather, energy can be focused on choices and solutions which move companies forward. Blame, shame, accusations-all of these attachment problems only create a lack of forward motion because they are leader-ego-centric. Instead, detachment equips the leader to make empowered decisions.

Additionally, detachment gives you space to receive and respect the input of others. You'll more readily see the flaws in a program or the misalignment of a goal because you're open to input of others who might have differing ideas from your own, who might see things from a different perspective. Even though a detached leader is much better at looking at the situation from a bird's eye view, that leader will still never see every flaw in every plan. Being open to the input of others who find the flaws in your plans is crucial in leadership but the mindset at the core is detaching from your own ideas. In this, the leader is detached enough to balance the confidence needed to present their own ideas with the maturity to detach from those ideas when those ideas may not work.

Sometimes leaders can be very passionate about their vision, their mission, and where they want to take an organization. But this passion, if taken to an extreme, can actually work against the leader. It can cause the leader to believe that their way and their vision is the only way, and, therefore, any dissonant ideas are simply anti-vision. They are right back to this whole I'm-right-and-you're-wrong mentality. Leaders who show up this way disrespectfully dismiss the input of others because their input clashes with the passion of the leader. Passion is not an excuse for acting like a jerk and being disrespectful.

BENEFITS OF DETACHMENT

There are many benefits to detachment that I've realized on a personal level as well. When I was going through the situation of experiencing the relapse of my husband, I did not know how to detach. First, I blamed myself for his choices and because I blamed myself, I swooped in and tried to solve them. This also, in part, lead to the belief that if I could understand more about addiction and his choices, if I could just know where he was, if I could get him to understand, then he would change. If I'm brutally honest, my identity was pretty wrapped up in his choices which kept me blind to my own. If only he would choose *my* idea for the best solution, everything would be fine. I was attached to what he did because I saw his choices as a part of my identity and what gave me security. This is common in many types of relationships, not just those where addiction is an issue.

Detachment gave me the freedom to relinquish control. It gave me the freedom to make choices that were in my own best interest, regardless of what his choices ended up being.

The detachment I began to create for myself between myself and my husband was not an indication of a lack of love. I cared very deeply for him and I still do now. The fear surrounding detachment for me at least, is I was afraid he would think I didn't care about him anymore and he would leave. Since then, I've learned I had an attachment to what people thought. I didn't want them to know how bad it was for him, and I didn't want a divorce. I didn't want another broken relationship. And my attachment, what I called love, was really all about me, even though I fooled myself into thinking it was about him. My inability to detach was really about protecting my ego, my reputation, being overly concerned about what people thought about me and him. It actually had nothing to do with loving him.

Detachment in this situation benefitted me greatly because it quieted the ego enough for me to actually take care of myself and gave me the capacity to love him appropriately in this circumstance. That choice became very important once he went into recovery. And trust me, just because a spouse is in recovery and living a vibrant recovery program, does not mean that detachment is still not necessary. Detachment is a mindset that I embrace on a daily basis. Is it challenging? Yes, less frequently than it used to be, but it's still challenging. There are always new opportunities for me to detach.

Detachment benefits me professional as well. One of

my most recent work experiences regarding detachment was when the organization I run went through a tremendous transition. There were many levels to that transition and one of the last parts of the transition was a change in leadership. Namely, me becoming the leader of the organization. In that transition, with the former leader leaving, the changes that occurred were very painful. Some were expected but many others, unexpected. The organization I run is a nonprofit and like all other nonprofits, we are funded through charitable giving as a primary revenue source. When this leadership change occurred, I expected attrition in giving and attendance to our events and programs. I expected this dip in finances and engagement. I thought I had detached. Nope!

The attrition was much greater than I ever anticipated, which created a myriad of financial problems for me to solve all within the first two years of being in this new role. I was not prepared for what I experienced emotionally and quickly learned how attached I was to the success of this organization.

I would love to tell you that even though I had learned the concept of detachment prior to this experience, I was able to detach from that situation and live happily ever after. Nope. At least, not at first. For roughly the first six to eight months of this difficult season, I didn't know it, but I was afraid I was going to ruin the organization. I saw the lack of revenue coming in. I saw the attendance wane at our events. And I completely blamed myself.

The thoughts swirling in my head were things like, "I'm ruining this organization that's been around for thirty years. This ship is going down on my watch. We have no money, and it's all my fault."

Let me tell you, I was heartbroken by what I perceived as my own professional failure, and I woke up every day in a puddle of anxiety. There were days I could not get out of bed, feeling anchored to the mattress by a thousand-pound anvil. And the days I managed to get out of bed, it took every ounce of energy to make it out of my house. I remember sitting in an appointment and afterwards rushing to my car so I could burst into tears.

Thankfully, I eventually started working with a coach. And while we never used the term detachment in our coaching, I realized about three weeks into that coaching experience what my primary issue was.

See, my core fear is that I'm going to have egg on my face; that something isn't going to work out, and I'm going to look bad. That fear is simply an attachment to a good outcome. What does that good outcome mean? Well, it means I did a good job, I'm a success, I'm not a failure. And while there's nothing wrong with wanting to achieve success and to not fail, I realized my ego was attached to that outcome; every big and little thing threatened that outcome and became debilitating to me. The opportunity before me was the chance to operate at yet another level of detachment. The process I used was the same process I'm preaching in this book, which is to start with awareness of the core thought, challenge that thought and choose something new supportive of what you want.

The goal wasn't for me to try to not be afraid. I was afraid of something going wrong and denying it would have been a futile effort. Naming the fear and just being aware of it gave way to the ability to identify the damaging thoughts I was having, many of which I've just shared. Thoughts like, "You're going to run this organization into the ground". Armed with detachment, I could make new choices around new thoughts that separated my worth from the organization's performance. When I did this, not only did my outlook change but I also showed up differently. I got creative and ended up writing new revenue-producing curriculum. At the end of that two-year period, we survived and even surpassed several goals.

ATTACH TO SOMETHING

The truth is, sometimes plans work out and sometimes they don't. When I was able to attach instead to my everyday efforts-something I can control-I began to take on what was in front of me for that day. What do I need to accomplish today at work? Who do I need to connect with today? Who do I need to talk to? What donor do I need to call back? Once I began to attach to what I had control over versus what the outcome might or might not be, I was amazed at the choices I began to see; choices that have put the organization in a much healthier financial position.

Attaching to our actions versus outcomes is simple when applied to everyday activities. For example: when I had a meeting with a potential client, instead of attaching to my desired outcome (the client hiring my nonprofit), I attached to my actions-what I could control (being prepared, running a good meeting and providing value). I repeated this approach day in and day out in order to get myself out of the grips of fear. Instead of fear of all the bad outcomes I could imagine, I redirected my energy to attaching to what I could control-the process, my actions, and efforts.

I don't ever want to repeat that difficulty again in my life because it was one of the most challenging lessons I've ever learned. I'm aware there will be a future with similar challenges, but I believe I'm better prepared-not because I have the right formula down to turn it around, but because I have the awareness. I have the mindset of detachment now. It might take me a couple days before I have the aha moment where I say, "Oh, wait a second, Shannon. You're attaching to something in an unhealthy way. You're in fear," or whatever the case may be. I'll get there.

These mindsets are not meant to create a pattern and process that, if you follow them one, two, three, you'll get the outcome that you want. To make that kind of claim would be antithetical to the point. I'm encouraging you to actually let go of outcomes. Detach from outcomes. Commit and work your plans but let go of what that work can create. I don't want you focused on your outcomes at all-not as an individual, not as a leader. Focus on your goals absolutely all day long but detach from what happens as a result of working your goals. Trust me, in that detached state, when one of those goals or outcomes goes awry, you'll be better equipped to pivot and make the next best decision.

SURRENDER VS DETACHMENT

Surrender and detachment can seem like similar mindsets. They are closely related but with an important distinction. Surrender is setting down a behavior. It's more about stopping the actions and thoughts that cause us to operate in controlling ways.

Detachment, then, is the emotional work of not picking up the surrendered behaviors again. You can surrender to outcomes and cease to attempt to control them outwardly-this is a tremendous step. But this does not mean you have detached emotionally from those outcomes.

Now, let's Identify, Challenge and Change.

IDENTIFY

- In what ways do you think you attach to your work, other people, and your own ideas?
- What bad thing will happen if you detach emotionally and develop a calm, nonreactive presence?

CHALLENGE

- Look at your answers from above. Are they true? Are any of your reasons for not changing, extreme thinking? What choices do you have?

CHANGE

- What will you focus on when you become aware of attachment so that you can detach appropriately in areas of struggle?

9
MINDSET FIVE
GRATITUDE: RECOGNIZING WHAT YOU VALUE

I am a firm believer that gratitude cannot be overdone. However, I fear gratitude has lost its true value due to a watered-down perception of the true nature and benefits of the practice of gratitude. Perhaps gratitude is taken for granted because of societal memes and suggestions such as, "have an attitude of gratitude" or the commonplace action of making gratitude lists. Can real gratitude be captured in a list I write for myself anyway? Does this honor the power of the act of being grateful? These are the questions in my mind as I ponder how a servant leader can adopt this mindset.

I want to be clear: creating gratitude lists and journaling about all there is to be thankful for is good. This good habit forces our minds to look for things to be thankful for in our everyday life-a particularly powerful tool when things are not going so well. I'm not suggesting these actions be eliminated.

However, I do want to make a case for the benefits of implementing gratitude as a *mindset* into everything that we do; into every experience we have, regardless of the outcomes and circumstances. In this, I believe the lists, journaling, and attitudes of gratitude only scratch the surface of this super, amazing mindset. In fact, of all the mindsets in this book, this is the one that takes the least amount of mind-shifting because of its compounding effects.

WHAT IS GRATITUDE?

Definitions around gratitude are pretty clear and basic: the act of being grateful...shocker. Being grateful, however, goes deeper and relates to having a warm and deep appreciation. I love that phrase, "A warm and deep appreciation." It makes me think of a warm blanket that is all encompassing that completely covers me. It's the perfect temperature that warms to the bone. Gratitude has a depth and warmth to it that moves beyond the cursory "thanks" to a more profound expression of appreciation.

Psychologists provide another way to define gratitude: a positive emotional response that we've perceived on giving or receiving a benefit from someone. (Kennon M. Sheldon 2011)(Edmonds and McCullough, 2004)

And yet one particular definition that caught my eye came from the dictionary and it reads, "the quality of being thankful; readiness to show appreciation for and *to return kindness.*"

To return kindness...that seems a bit more active than making a gratitude list or saying "thanks," doesn't it? For the purposes of this chapter, think of gratitude as the overriding mindset related to being thankful by expressing deep, warm appreciation and to return kindness. With this in mind, you will notice I interchange all of these terms.

WHY IS GRATITUDE IMPORTANT?

Not that this is news, but gratitude is healthier, and it feels better. It's a natural antidepressant. Gratitude has been shown to create dopamine and serotonin in both the giver and receiver. Dopamine and serotonin are those feel-good neurotransmitters in the brain. Additionally, scientists have studied neural pathways in our brain and say we can build new ones by a process called neuroplasticity.

Neural pathways are formed when cells in the brain talk to each other a lot. The more the same communication between cells takes place, the faster more embedded the pathway becomes. (Chowdhury 2019) Brains like be to super-efficient and when the communication becomes fast enough, the process becomes automatic. The more automatic our thoughts are, the more likely we are unaware of them-they are living in our subconscious. In action, these neural pathways help us form habits. A habit for the most part, is the outward expression of a proficient thought pattern in the brain. These neural pathways can be changed! But not without effort.

Neuroplasticity is the ability of the brain to learn new pathways. What's exciting is we can create these new pathways on purpose. But changing neuropathways doesn't come easy. As mentioned earlier in this book, changing the way we think requires a high level of awareness and a willingness to be wrong, a willingness to change, a willingness to grow. It requires a commitment to the possibility of experiencing a little growth pain because hey, when I find out I'm wrong, it doesn't feel good.

But what's cool about gratitude is that it's one of the few changes we can make in our neural pathways that is less painful because of those amazing feel-good hormones, dopamine and serotonin. In short, if you struggle with gratitude, meaning you struggle with really feeling it, that is just a neural pathway that can be improved with use. And with some effort, you can practice more gratitude and get some good feelings right away, making it more likely to create a new neural pathway for you.

Gratitude is also important because it is a recognition of what we value and recognizing that value in word and in deed. This recognition can be applied to circumstances, not just people. In fact, as gratitude grows naturally as a mindset, it begins looking for things to appreciate all around; things like nature, other people, big and small gestures, and even pain. Yes, gratitude can help you find the good in pain without "silver-lining" your experience. This is where I notice a strong relationship between servant leadership and gratitude.

When I recognize what I value in something or someone, I need a degree of humility and even vulnerability to do so. Gratitude becomes a recognition someone did something that I benefited from and that I am not afraid to point it out. This recognition is an admission I need that person. To say, "I need you", for some of us, is one of the most difficult things we can say. Talk about humility.

Gratitude is also important because, interestingly enough, it's a way to stay in the present moment. Gratitude is a recognition that something has or is bringing us something good that we are noticing, right now. Sure, we could be grateful for something in our past. Absolutely. Fortunately, there are no negative ramifications of being grateful for the past. A lot of our damage and focusing on the past is not when we're looking back with gratitude, but when we're looking back with shame, regret or even fear. But using gratitude as we look to the past is a positive thing. In the present, gratitude has the potential to bring us joy, right now, today, because we can recognize something that's happening in the current moment.

Additionally, gratitude aids in changed perspectives when challenges arise. Life is full of ups and downs, as everybody knows. And, as discussed previously, some of life is positive, some of life is negative. Understanding and accepting both positive and negative is an important, healthy step in our mental capacity. When the challenges of life arise, gratitude is a powerful antidote. My tendency is to hyper-focus on the bad, like a magnifying glass, making it much bigger than it needs to be. When things are not going well in my life, when I'm feeling particularly challenged, it's like my brain can only see the negative. I'm sure there's science behind this, but my mind tends to shut down all of the good and zero in on the bad, and all the good becomes nonexistent.

We can experience this in circumstances but also in

how we view ourselves. For example, when I used to make mistakes at work, I would literally say out loud, "Shannon, you are so stupid. You can't do anything right!"

Now, while my old self talk could be related to a whole different problem, one thing is for sure, the difficulty I experienced was so strong and so powerful that my brain was only able to see the negative and compounded it into a completely irrational statement like, "I'm stupid and I can't do anything right." Neither of those statements is true at all. Neither of those statements is accurate of my performance as a professional. Yet in that moment, I believed them to be absolute truth. Gratitude helps me to right-size my problems by recognizing what I learned from the mistake, what choices I have about moving forward, and the experience I've gained as a result.

I am not suggesting we silver-line our experiences, which is basically ignoring the bad to avoid experiencing the negative. Rather, gratitude gives me more balance and allows me to see my problems for what they are by not magnifying them, not ignoring them, and acknowledging the gifts in the midst of those problems. This is simply an act of looking for the good without magnifying or denying the bad.

Finally, gratitude is also important because it supports the desired culture and environment of servant leadership. Part of the responsibility of servant leaders is to model desirable behavior so the culture on our team and/or organizations can thrive. If the leader wants a culture of appreciation and gratitude, they must model it for others and discourage or even disallow behavior that works against gratitude.

As a leader, do I want most of the people at work to feel like gratitude is not available and only happening in pockets of the company? Or, do I want just a few people at work to feel like outsiders when they are not showing up in gratitude? I pick the latter. I know it's not realistic that every person working for me will take my modeled behavior and adopt it as their own. But I do want the overall culture of my organization to be one where a lack of gratitude is the exception, not the rule.

I set the tone for appropriateness as the leader. If I'm angry, difficult to work with, cussing people out, then guess what? Those around me are going to think those responses to conflict are welcomed. But instead, if my response to conflict is gratitude, then my brain will not only look for the good, it will find it. If my response is to problem-solve, to not point the finger and blame, then I get curious about what can be done about a situation. If my response is to find and share lessons, then I am modeling the kind of culture that is okay around me and by default, my organization. This commitment to gratitude creates space to solve problems by seeing a situation in its totality, not just according to what went wrong.

I want my modeling of gratitude to be so ingrained in my organization-and even in my personal relationships-that other people simply do not feel comfortable acting any other way around me.

Gratitude encourages the desired behaviors that we have for the people who work for us. It goes beyond just saying, "Thanks for completing that report." Gratitude, because of its specificity and because it comes from a deep-seated appreciation for what other people have done for you and for your organization, is basically like saying to people, "Yes, do more of that. I like that." I maintain that most of us humans are sponges for acceptance and validation. Gratitude provides this validation and this acceptance to the people around you.

CREATING MORE DEPTH

Moving beyond the lists and thank-you's is not hard, but it does take a deeper understanding of the ways we can practice the mindset of gratitude.

First, we must start with the belief that people matter and are worthy of being deeply and warmly appreciated. This depth is good for them, good for us, and good for our organizations.

Second, we have to move past being *for* gratitude and

being *bold* about it. This is a commitment to make gratitude a part of our daily life, both personally and professionally.

Finally, we must promote this new way of thinking in our organizations by both modeling and operationalizing it into our cultures. There are a few ways this can be done both in thinking and doing.

Meaning Not Just Manners

I see it all the time: leaders implement acts of gratitude or appreciation towards their associates in the form of recognition lunches, rewards programs, and discount clubs. There's nothing wrong with broad, organization-wide programs like these. However, I don't believe they fit the definitions of gratitude previously given.

My concern is these programs become a cookie-cutter one-size-fits-all act of appreciation. They do not require the leadership to actually *engage in gratitude*. So instead of being special, or tailored to wants and needs, these "gifts" are related to getting the most bang for the organizational buck, a shot across the bow. The motivation is not gratitude, the motivation is more along the lines of manners and maybe protocol.

Listen, I'm a fan of manners. It's nice and proper to thank people. Let's not stop doing this. But I think we can do better. I think we can do more.

We can establish a culture of gratitude by:

- Showing gratitude in ways that are meaningful to the other person
- Getting specific about what we are grateful for
- Connecting *what* we are grateful for, to *why* we are grateful for it

Equitable Expression

Because you're a leader, your deep, warm expression of gratitude has a greater impact. I believe this is true because everything a leader says and does holds more weight simply because they are the leader. I found this out the hard way when I went from being a teacher to an elementary principal; I became the boss of my co-workers. I learned fast how much my expression of gratitude, or the lack thereof, impacted the teachers who worked for me. It was easy to express warm appreciation for the people I liked. It was natural then, to inadvertently share deep appreciation with some but not others. I learned I had to be more equitable in my displays of appreciation, whether or not someone was my "cup of tea."

Why? Because the impact of my lack of appreciation and gratitude actually created a negative impact on people. Withholding appreciation is not neutral…it does harm. I don't want that, and any caring leader wouldn't want that either.

To work on this, I had to dial up my appreciation towards some and dial back for others. This isn't a perfect science but more of an awareness of my tendency to play favorites. Note: If you are someone who purposefully withholds appreciation and gratitude to punish others, you are hurting yourself. Yes, you are punishing the other person, but remember this: when your people are winning, you win too. But when you create the negative environment of losing by intentionally withholding this kind of deep appreciation, your people lose and therefor you lose. You'll never tap into their discretionary effort, which is what we all want.

Overdo Appreciation

When you think you're expressing the right amount of gratitude, chances are that the people around you are just beginning to experience it. In other words, more than likely, it's not enough. Carolyn Wiley of Roosevelt University conducted a study about appreciation in the workplace. (Heath 2017) This study spanned forty-six years and included surveying employees and their supervisors about their top motivations at work. In those forty-six years Carolyn found that only two motivating factors showed up every time the survey was conducted. One of them was "full appreciation of work done." Of course, they asked supervisors if they had expressed appreciation and then asked the subordinates if they had felt appreciated. When asking supervisors, eighty percent reported they showed appreciation to their direct reports, but only twenty percent of their direct reports said they *felt appreciated* by their supervisors. This was not only a surprise to those who took part in the study, but a huge surprise to me. If you think you are showing appreciation and gratitude to the people around you, both at home and at work, you might be doing an okay job, but do more. Chances are, it's just not enough.

A Common Mistake

Many leaders want to know when enough is enough. How do we know how much is enough gratitude? My question is...*enough for what*? If we are showing gratitude to create a reaction or awareness in another person, it's not gratitude, it's manipulation. What we are really doing is wearing the trappings of gratitude in order to serve our own selfish need to be validated. That kind of expression is from a needy energy, not an energy of actually showing gratitude. I show gratitude whenever I feel it, regardless if the person responds in kind or not. It's not about a response and you are never really finished because there's always something to express gratitude for.

BUT WHAT IF PEOPLE DON'T DESERVE GRATITUDE?

Not everyone who works for us hits the ball out of the park. Sometimes the lack of performance is a training issue, hiring issue or other circumstances completely outside our control. One of the biggest mistakes leaders make, however, is withholding gratitude from those who have low performance as a form of punishment or for fear the poor performance continues. Remember: withholding gratitude, even if unintentional, has a diminishing effect on people around us. I can think of no one in greater need of gratitude and appreciation than the person struggling at work. Am I suggesting we express gratitude specifically for the poor work performance? No. I am saying that deep, specific appreciation can be useful in connecting to someone who is performing below standards. This balanced feedback becomes a mechanism for creating those feel-good responses while also delivering pieces of information harder to discuss.

In this, the leader operates with a *mindset* of gratitude; the leader is getting good at finding and expressing areas worthy of recognition while providing necessary feedback for improvement. Besides, their performance can't be all bad. If it is, why are they still an employee? Have you considered that someone else's poor performance is a mindset issue? Are you more equipped to help them through it using the tools of gratitude as well as the other mindsets?

WHERE TO BEGIN?

I always recommend starting with yourself. I do something most nights as I fall asleep. You don't need a pen or paper or even an electronic device unless you like to record these things. If you want to start a gratitude journal, go for it. I started recording mine on a piece of paper, but eventually I grew tired of that and I just rehearse it my head now. I call it my three, three, and three and it's pretty simple.

I think of three things from that day that went well, and I name them in my head. Then I think of three things that day that didn't go well, that I'd like to focus on doing better tomorrow or the next time they present themselves (more on that concept in Chapter 10). And then, I finish with three things I'm grateful for from that day. The caveat: the three things I'm grateful for cannot be the three things that went well. Why? My goal is to really end my day with six things that were positive, while never forgetting that it's important to do a little inventory and never ignore the things that didn't go well. This ensures I don't silver-line my days and ignore opportunities for improvement and growth.

Balancing Feedback

Moving beyond the personal to the workplace, the three, three and three is a great model for engaging with others. For example, if you are having a meeting with someone where you are finding it hard to recognize the good, the three, three, and three can help you prepare. State three specific and personal things they are doing well; ask them to identify three areas of challenge or improvement. Work together collaboratively as a team to help and develop strategies and ideas for improving on those three things. Then finish with three things you are grateful for, related to that person. This is a great way to engage that mindset of vulnerability and to really close the loop with the mindset of gratitude.

Get Specific

All too often, our show of appreciation towards others is too generic and curt, creating an unintentional perception of being disingenuous. Getting specific means, we name what we are thankful for in that person or what we are appreciative of. Then, telling the other person what their job well done means to *us*, what it helped *us* accomplish, and what it means to the team, the organization, the vision. Tie the specific gratitude to as big of an impact as you can without being disingenuous.

Make it Personal

Making it personal is taking the time to say someone's name (or write it in the email); it involves tying the feedback to *their* personal and/or professional goals. Additionally, making it personal means you think about the benefits and payoffs of their behavior and you express how you believe those benefits come into play.

Schedule Gratitude

This may seem silly but making time on your calendar to show gratitude through deep appreciation may be the only way you get it into your everyday routine. I know that sounds strange but trust me on this. Scheduling time to appreciate others will ensure you express gratitude often and make it a part of your everyday activities. Any new behavior seems to take more time at first, but once you make this new action a habit, showing appreciation can become another step in your daily or weekly routine.

There's a company in my hometown that created a strategy for showing appreciation for and recognizing the efforts of one another. They created a playbook of actions supportive of company culture, organized by their values. One of their values was gratitude. In the gratitude section of the playbook, were several pages of ideas the associates could pick from at any time, to show gratitude. One of the ideas in the playbook was as follows: When you arrive at work, send three emails to three different people telling each one what you are grateful for from them, from the day before.

I absolutely love this idea! The communications were short, one or two sentence emails taking less than five minutes to accomplish. The leaders began to notice that employees were actually looking for things throughout the day to show gratitude for the next morning before they started their work.

Now think about this from the perspective of what has been shared in this chapter. The leadership created a playbook outlining not just values and culture but strategies, tactics, and even expectations for living out those values. This employer prioritized gratitude by placing it in their playbook. Then, by utilizing that playbook idea, employees were exercising gratitude in alignment with the culture, creating feel-good hormones in their brain while building new neural pathways through this repeated behavior and ultimately, making it almost unacceptable to be ungrateful at work. All with a playbook! They understood it wasn't enough to state that they value gratitude, they needed to operationalize it. You can do this for yourself and your team too!

IDENTIFY

What gets in the way of adopting a mindset of gratitude? Here are some common pushbacks:
- I don't know what the payoffs/impacts of achieving goals are for my team.
- I don't have time.
- Their work is so bad! I don't want to encourage poor performance.
- I show appreciation by making sure they get paid every week.
- I can't find gratitude in myself.

CHALLENGE

I don't believe most people resist the idea of gratitude or even the idea that it is a good thing to do. And yet, based on studies, leaders do a really poor job in executing appreciation for others. Looking at your own reasons for not adopting this mindset and some of the examples above and begin to challenge them.

Truth
- Do you really not have time or are you just not making gratitude a priority?

Extremes
- Is it extreme to think if you show gratitude to someone who's a low performer that they're going to continue performing low? Does that seem a little extreme?

Responsibility
- Whose job is it to create an encouraging and gracious or gratitude-filled environment? Isn't that the leader's job? Are you the leader? Doesn't that make it your job?

Choices
- If so, what part of that are you not taking responsibility for that you should start taking responsibility for now?
- And finally, as you move forward with this new awareness what choices do you have? What choice will you make?

CHANGE

When you identify all the choices you actually have, I hope you start with yourself. You can choose to develop this mindset in yourself. You can choose to be more intentional, personal, and specific with your gratitude to others. You can set aside time on your calendar to do these things, so they aren't left up to happenstance. When you make your choice, I encourage you, as always, to choose to embrace this mindset of gratitude and to employ some of the tactics even if it's just one. The one-two punch of thinking differently and doing differently is what brings about the most amount of change.

INTEGRATION

10
TAKING INVENTORY

Taking a personal inventory is something a lot of people think of as an end of life process. As people near death or the end of their lives, they may review the person they were, their actions, relationships, attitudes, and beliefs. Taking stock of our history and choices towards the end of our lives can be useful, but in a way…possibly a little too late. I believe the practice of taking a personal inventory doesn't need to be relegated only to those close to death.

I first heard of taking a personal inventory when I learned more about twelve step programs. Part of my healing and recovery when I experienced my husband's relapse was entering into a twelve-step program of my own. While this chapter is not meant to duplicate or even borrow concepts from the twelve steps, the wisdom of taking a personal inventory is found in those steps. And, upon further investigation, the insights around taking inventory are found among many other traditions and practices around the world. For this reason, taking inventory of ourselves is a worthy endeavor if we are committed to both personal and professional growth.

Our growth as human beings is never done. We're

always evolving, whether it's from a cellular level all the way to how we think. But when it comes to personal development, our commitment to growth can slow and even cease without awareness. It's in that commitment to growth where we can experience problems in both personal and professional transformation. Like our physical growth, especially when we were adolescents, growth comes in spurts. There are times we experience personal and professional growth where we feel like we are growing leaps and bounds, and then other times we feel like we have reached a plateau. So, just because we aren't growing this very moment, doesn't mean our commitment to growth has waned. However, if we aren't careful, we can fall victim to the thinking that growth should be steady, constant, and linear.

Think about what happens on a weight-loss diet. Many people get discouraged with diets because they fail to realize their natural progression. A well-balanced diet doesn't result in steady weight loss over time; rather, results in initial water weight loss, then a slowing of loss and then a plateau. If the dieter remains steady on their plan, eventually that plateau is broken. Sometimes, the dieter temporarily gains a few pounds too. This is all a part of the process. But if the dieter is unaware of this normal dynamic of losing weight, they may become discouraged.

In similar fashion, personal and even professional growth is the same. In fact, growth might mean that we improve for a while, maybe take a couple of steps back, make a huge leap a little later on, and then maybe regress a little bit. That's okay. The goal of personal and professional growth really is to make progress towards improvement over the span of our life, understanding growth is not linear. Just like in dieting, we will have "fits and starts" that, in the midst of them, may look like we are backtracking or failing. In reality, these steps are all a part of the overall improvement and growth in our lives.

Sometimes, growth can look like a huge aha moment, and then other times might feel stagnant. In the midst of the aha's or giant leaps, it is common to believe that experience is what all change and development feels and looks like, so our expectations are set pretty high. Instead if we can view these highs and these lows in their right context-that they are both a part of the process-we can relax into the personal and professional growth experience. Commitment to the growth process and a willingness to change are key, even if changes are not felt on a regular basis.

Most professionals conduct a workplace inventory of sorts, right? Like an annual assessment or, if you're like me, a mid-year informal assessment and a year-end formal assessment. Your job might even ask you to conduct a self-inventory or a self-assessment. If you're working on a project at work, you probably review metrics throughout the process and look for certain trends while assessing setbacks and achievements alike.

There doesn't seem to be a set self-measurement tool that everyone agrees on for personal growth or really even for professional growth. There are many tools, and each have their own merit. Personally, I've used too many personal and professional assessment tools to count. But interestingly enough, I've learned from them all. So, I'm a fan and encourage you to seek out those formal assessment tools on your own.

I'd rather equip you with some tools to enable you to do your own self-inventory on a regular basis to ensure you keep awareness at the forefront of your mind. Please know you'll never get all the insight you need by yourself. Nothing beats the mirror reflection of a coach, boss or significant other telling you about your own bullshit.

While taking a personal and professional self-inventory is not going to be sufficient for getting you to understand all there is to know about yourself-if that's even possible-a regular personal inventory is something that will put you light years ahead of those who don't do any self-inventory at all and will keep the primary catalyst of change at the forefront of your life: awareness.

Successful people take personal inventory regularly. People who are prone to repetitive and unnecessary failure-because not all failure is bad, and some failure is necessary-are failing mostly due to an inability or unwillingness to rigorously look at themselves and then correct course. For the purposes of this book, taking an inventory is about taking time to think about who you are and how you're showing up. In other words, it's an intentional self-awareness that we set aside time for. All of us can tend towards the mistake of operating on autopilot, going in and out of our days unaware of our own attitudes, personality traits and fears impacting our decisions and outcomes. Creating a habit of regular self-inventory gently encourages us to evaluate our results and attitudes and therefore bring about change by preventing new undesirable habits

Self-scrutiny can be extremely painful, however. For most of us, looking at ourselves and then realizing we messed up doesn't feel very good. Self-scrutiny or a self-inventory is essentially entering into a process of a willingness to be wrong.

Ask yourself this question right now. Are you willing to be wrong? It sounds easy at first but think about the implications. There are beliefs you have right this very moment that you believe to be "gospel" truth and they are completely true for you...and only you. They are one hundred percent created in your thoughts. That's it.

A willingness to being wrong allows us to challenge what can be called a "truth ceiling." I first heard this phrase from Master Coach, Brooke Castillo. While the concept of a truth ceiling is not new, the imagery of a ceiling seemed novel and very helpful to me.

A truth ceiling is a belief equated with fact, meaning, we don't question whether the thing we believe is true or not. We just assume it is. These types of truth ceilings come in a couple different forms.

First, a truth ceiling can be a belief generally accepted by others or even society as a whole. In this instance, we never really consider something other than our belief about a certain topic could be true. For example: most people believe the earth is round. This is a generally accepted truth (although there are those who argue against this belief today), but there was a time this was not the case. There was a time most of humanity believed the earth was flat. This was a truth ceiling. What's interesting is even though people believed the earth was flat, their belief didn't mean the earth being round was impossible!

At one time people didn't believe it was possible to communicate over this thing called a telephone. Also, a truth ceiling. What about texting and the internet? All of these advancements in technology nobody believed were true. You could say they all had truth ceilings. Just because a truth ceiling at one point in history told us the only way to communicate was through telegraph, didn't mean texting wasn't possible!

Your truth ceilings have little to do with possibility.

For most of us, the truth ceilings that are hurting us aren't the scientific ones, rather the ones that are of our own thinking in relationship to our personality, our emotions, values, preferences and life circumstances. Challenging truth ceilings allows us the room to be wrong about the things we once believed. Sometimes a truth ceiling can show up in terms of what we believe about other people or something we've experienced. We accept it as truth but it's not really true. This is why it's important to challenge for truth, extremes, responsibility, and choices as much as we can. When we don't challenge our beliefs, we end up becoming stagnant in our growth. One of the ways to continually challenge our truth ceilings or our beliefs, is a regular self-inventory. (The Life Coach School 2019)

But how do we self-evaluate ourselves on more of a micro-level, maybe even on a daily basis, to ensure we're not forming new unproductive habits or limiting truth ceilings? If you remember in the last chapter when I talked about the concept of neural pathways, I briefly explained how those neural pathways are formed. While we can form new neural pathways, we can unknowingly strengthen old ones if we're not really intentional about evaluating ourselves on a regular basis.

Taking a personal self-inventory isn't just painful because we may be wrong about something; this approach can induce pain because we may realize we are not as far along as we thought in our personal or professional development journey. What this looked like for me was having a personal aha moment and then realizing months later, I had to relearn the lesson professionally. As a result, I was totally shocked and taken completely off-guard.

My difficulties on the job became an opportunity to apply something I had learned previously through my husband's relapse. One of the biggest lessons I learned out of that experience that I'm so grateful for today, was understanding more about what surrender looks like, how it benefits me, and how it helps me to deal with, lessen, and eliminate unnecessary fears. You'd think that after such a strong experience, I would never have had to learn that lesson again.

Not so.

WHERE TO FOCUS PERSONAL SELF-INVENTORY

When taking my own self-inventory, I focus on four main areas: Habits, values, personality traits and wants and needs.

Habits: What are the repetitive things I'm doing I'm not happy with or that I want to change?

Values: What are the values that I want to live by? And have I, in any way, violated those values recently?

Personality: What parts of my personality don't serve me well and how pronounced are those traits? Am I making choices in alignment with the kind of person I want to be?

Wants and Needs: What do I want and need and in what ways have I sabotaged and/or ignored these?

Habits

Habits can be productive and destructive. Not all habits are bad. I like to ask myself about any habits that are destructive. These habits don't have to be destructive in some major way either. They can simply be habits that keep me from what I really want. For example, while writing this book, I had a destructive habit of putting off the next step in my writing process. Once I realized I had a habit of procrastinating about the thing I wanted the most (to write a book), I got honest about my motivations and discovered why I was putting off this big goal. Bottom line: I needed to become aware of my habits to challenge and change them. When you take an inventory of your habits, it's important to not only think about the things that you do repetitively that you're aware of, but also to get really honest about the things that you're not aware of.

So how does one become honest about what they *are unaware of*? This seems impossible but bear with me. I'll use my procrastination habit. In order to break the habit of putting off the thing I wanted the most, I needed to get to my core thinking. *In thinking about my thinking, I brought the unconscious to my consciousness*...I started the process of awareness by thinking through the Hula Hoop model. Unproductive actions are created by damaging feelings. Damaging feelings are created by limiting thoughts. And limiting thoughts come from the meaning I have placed on an event or circumstance.

So what meaning was I placing on the writing process? What was I believing to be true? Here are some thoughts I discovered:

- Writing is hard.
- I've never written a book before.
- No one is going to read my book.
- No one will like my book.
- Other people have written books about mindset and awareness. This is nothing special so why bother?

As you can imagine, the limiting thoughts above did not create desirable feelings. They were limiting thoughts and so they created damaging feelings. And guess what? They resulted in unproductive actions that over time, became unproductive habits. Well no wonder! Thinking thoughts like "No one will read my book." and "Why bother?" aren't exactly going to create feelings of excitement, motivation and joy, the feelings usually needed for a creative process.

My awareness truly started in my results. What were my results? Not a chapter written as a result of procrastination. If I wanted different results, I needed new thoughts and it all started with getting honest about what I was really thinking.

Another way to get more aware of unconscious habits is to notice feelings. Am I having a normal negative feeling or is it a damaging feeling? All of the thoughts about writing my book created damaging feelings, not just negative ones. And although this is just one example, the premise is to get better at noticing feelings and figuring out if they are damaging. How do I know if a feeling is damaging to me? It creates unproductive habits-habits that don't give me the results I want. To help me feel my feelings, I started a little record of my feelings on a notepad. At the end of each day, I made note of any icky feelings and traced them back to my thoughts and figured out if they were resulting in any unproductive habits. If not, they were just a run-of-the-mill negative feeling. We get these, it's okay. But if feelings were causing unproductive habits, I drank the Kool-Aid and began to use my own method of Identify, Challenge and Change.

As I kept doing this, I started noticing some patterns. My unproductive habit of procrastination showed up in other areas too. I also began to understand a lot of my past and was able to give myself a little grace and forgiveness. I didn't know better then. I do now.

Values

I'm a fan of having personal values but just a few. I have five main values, but I focus on really aligning as often as I can with my top three. I do this because I have found if I'm living in alignment with those top three as a minimum, I'm significantly more content and fulfilled. My aim is progress, not perfection. I've provided a values list here (Fig. 9), check it out.

This list is not exhaustive but will give you a good start at really thinking about what's important to you. Take a look at the list and check the values that just seem to call to you. For this first pass, don't worry about checking too many. Then, take those that you checked and narrow them down to five. No need to categorize them or put them in order of importance. Once you have your top five, pick your top three in order of importance. One, two, three.

VALUES LIST	
ACCEPTANCE	JOY
ACCOMPLISHMENT	JUSTICE
AMBITION	KINDNESS
ASSERTIVENESS	KNOWLEDGE
BALANCE	LEADERSHIP
BEAUTY	LOGIC
BRAVERY	LOVE
CALM	LOYALTY
CANDOR	MATURITY
CHARITY	MEANING
COMMUNICATION	MOTIVATION
CURIOSITY	OPENNESS
DETERMINATION	OPTIMISM
DIGNITY	ORIGINALITY
DRIVE	PEACE
ENDURANCE	PLAYFULNESS
ENERGY	POWER
EXPLORATION	QUALITY
FAMILY	RECREATION
FAIRNESS	RESTRAINT
FREEDOM	SATISFACTION
GENEROSITY	SELF-RELIANCE
GOODNESS	SIGNIFICANCE
GROWTH	SILENCE
HONOR	SOLITUDE
HOPE	TEMPERANCE
HUMILITY	TOUGHNESS
IMAGINATION	TRUTH
INTEGRITY	UNDERSTANDING
IRREVERENT	WONDER

Figure 9

By the way, your values will change as your life changes, so be flexible; you don't have to stick with these the rest of your life. The benefit of knowing what you value personally helps you to then self-evaluate how much you are living in alignment with those values. The self-evaluation also helps to identify gaps. Where are you not experiencing or living in alignment with certain value in your life? And then eventually you can start finding ways to bring more of that value into your everyday life. But you will not be aware until you know what your values are, and you start evaluating your life against them.

As a leader, values alignment is crucial to creating and maintaining a culture. But listing values versus living values are two different things. To help yourself and your team live the values, there must be metrics and examples of how those values are operationalized. Just like the organization that created the playbook, you've got to figure out a way to both model values and hold people accountable to them and you can't hold people accountable to an undefined word on a poster in your hallway at work. A dear friend of mine, Jason Barger, author of *Thermostat Cultures* says this: "We put our posters on the wall but are the posters *in* us?" A self-inventory asks you to look at how well you are aligning with your values, not just if you have values identified.

Personality Traits

I've heard it said many times, people at their core do not change. I don't believe this. This is a victim mentality allowing for a lack of introspection and work on self. Sure, there are parts of my personality that may never change. I have no idea-check with me in thirty years.

There are certainly parts of my personality that I can honestly admit do not serve me well. In that awareness I can make new choices around my thoughts, feelings and actions and science tells me, those choices create new neural pathways. Those new neural pathways make a "new me" in those areas. Is that personality? I'm not one hundred percent sure. But I don't believe we're stuck with our most destructive personality traits. Caveat: there are certain mental and maybe even cognitive disorders that affect the personality. My statements are not clinical, nor do they pertain to those needing medical and/or clinical interventions to manage truly destructive personality traits; rather, people without acute disorders who tend to avoid personal growth through victim statements like, "Well you can't change your personality." Bullshit. You can change at least some of it. Why not try?

Wants and Needs

When I coach individuals and ask the question, "What do you want?", I am amazed at the answers or the lack thereof. Most people cannot tell me what they want; they've been too busy thinking about other people's wants and needs. So, I listen and ask again. Typically, the client cannot get to the core of what they want or what they want is for someone or something else to change. Now I realize that wants and needs are different, but I group them together because I believe the process of identifying them and moreover, why we do not, is the same. Getting to the core of what we want and need can be a scary process. But why are we so afraid?

Expressing wants and needs can be painful and fear-filled because by default, we are admitting there's a void, there's something missing. So instead of identifying what's missing in the form of an acknowledged need, it's easier to just not want the thing or pretend we don't need something. Afterall, if we ignore the want and it remains unmet, we won't be disappointed, right? In short, we avoid clarity around wants and needs for fear we won't get them and so we skirt the whole process. In this, saying what we want and need feels pretty risky.

Sometimes we know what we want and need but we deny it in the moment to please someone else. Sure, sometimes in life sacrifices are necessary. But I don't believe we have to default to sacrifice to prove something, rather, we can *choose* to sacrifice consciously. If you find yourself resentful towards others who you sacrifice for, chances are, your sacrificing has been at the expense of self without really deciding, *do I want to do this?* When our first thought is, "I have to do this and such or else," we are playing the victim and not exercising our right to choose our actions. Is there anything wrong with choosing to not meet one of your needs or wants for the benefit of someone else? Nothing wrong with this at all. But please allow me to encourage you to *make this choice consciously* after considering other choices. Just be sure you can do so without becoming angry or forming a resentment. Go right ahead and do that thing for your friend or family member. Before I showed up this way, I believed it to be selfish, bad or even sinful if I didn't help and do for others all the time. This was my servant leader truth ceiling. No wonder I felt frustrated all the time. I really didn't believe I had any choices.

I've sacrificed my own wants and needs for others repeatedly. There were many times when my kids were younger, I put off buying a new outfit for myself because they needed new school clothes, even if my jeans were threadbare or shoe soles were worn out. There just wasn't enough money to go around. I didn't make those sacrifices and then become resentful as a result. Instead, I chalked these choices up to part of being a parent. I've gotten older as have my children, and while they're all self-sufficient, there are times they've come to me and asked for a little extra cash. Now, the first thing I do is check in with myself and decide if I *want* to give them this money. How will I feel about giving my adult child this money? Will I be resentful? Will I wish I hadn't done it? Am I okay with any sacrifices that I might need to make in order to spend this money on them? This doesn't mean I'm against sacrificing for others. It does mean I need to think about sacrifice before engaging in it automatically. In doing so, I no longer get to play the victim. When I find myself mad about something, I did for someone and blaming that person, that's a huge red flag that I did something against what I really wanted or needed and that's one hundred percent on me.

Now, you might think that's overthinking things with my children. But for me, it's very important to think critically about what I want to do with my money and what my current financial needs are. When being asked to donate extra, help my son with a car repair or participate in a friend's online hostess party, I first ask myself if I can afford to spend the money (will any of my needs go unmet by spending this money?). I then ask if I *want* to spend it (what other wants will go by the wayside if I say yes to this expense?). Then I choose based on my financial needs and what I want to accomplish financially.

Money is not the only place we struggle to get clear about what we want and need. Take your 'time' for a moment. Have you ever been invited to a party, a family get-together, an event at school or church, where deep down you just did not want to be there? Maybe you didn't feel like being around people or maybe you knew there was going to be a certain experience that you weren't going to like, but you went anyway. As a result of going, you became angry and resentful; maybe towards yourself or worse, towards whoever invited you.

Why do that to yourself? What's so bad about just saying, "No thanks"? Saying "no" is one of the choices you have as an adult. Sometimes we forget that we have the freedom to make these kinds of choices. I know why we don't do this. I know why we say "yes" when inside we feel a resounding "no." We are afraid of what people will think. Listen to me: I do not choose based on whether or not someone will be let down, offended or hurt by my response. This is in essence, making their emotional environment more important than mine…which is also, putting my needs last. One of the ways I honor my wants and needs is I decide what is best for me and communicate my response to others in a kind way. I don't need to defend my answer or avoid the truth to enable others emotionally. Their response is theirs. Period.

I believe each of us inherently knows what we want and need. Ensuring we take care of those wants and needs makes us that much more able to meet the wants and needs of others. It's a servant leader move to address your own wants and needs first, just like grabbing the oxygen mask on the airplane before helping others. When I take a personal inventory around wants and needs, I'm looking for areas I compromised to please another person without thinking of my choices first. It's okay to compromise a want or need but let's make that choice consciously.

PUTTING IT INTO PRACTICE

What does taking an inventory look like in real life? Starting with the three, three and three gratitude practice is helpful. The second 'three' was about reflecting on three things that didn't go well that day. Those three things can be my own attitudes, thoughts, behaviors and damaging feelings. The key is, to focus my thinking on *myself*. In other words, the self-reflection is about what you can change.

Looking back on my day to reflect on three things that didn't go well isn't an opportunity to beat myself up. This is part of the reason the limit is three. I can tend to make a much larger list and start feeling pretty shitty about myself.

Instead, think of the inventory as a kind, friendly observer, looking over the day. *Hmmm, did I experience any damaging emotions? Interesting. Do I regret anything I said? Got it. Did I believe limiting thoughts? Oh, I see.* In the beginning, I used to write all of this down just as a matter of discipline and to get into the habit. Now, I just do it all in my head.

Then the next day or in the coming days, I get intentional about the things I've identified so when similar response begin to emerge in me, I am reminded of how I want to show up differently. Just this little awareness every evening before I go to bed has caused me to grow leaps and bounds in my thinking and in the ways I behave, as it keeps continuous improvement at the forefront of my life.

In taking inventory and looking at what went well and didn't go well, I'm allowing myself the space to grow and improve tomorrow. I'm intentionally giving my brain experience with being wrong and admitting that wrong to myself. But what about admitting my wrong to others, if appropriate? What if I realize I acted in a way that was not aligned with my values, my culture at work or even with what I want and need?

You always have choices about how you respond to what you discover in your inventory. As long as it will not cause more harm to a person, I strongly suggest making any wrongs, right. This isn't just an apology, however. This is admitting to the person you know you did something wrong and you ask how you can make it up to them. You make an amend, not an apology. This is how relationships have a chance at reconciliation. An apology is just words. An amend gives the other person power over you to determine next steps. An apology says, "I'm sorry." An amend says, "I see what I did, I can imagine how it hurt you. How can I make it right?" Big difference. Apology = words. Amend = actions.

Starting a Self-Inventory

Whether you choose the three, three and three as a part of your inventory or something more or less formal, I suggest you establish a routine of at least asking yourself what went wrong that day that you'd like to change. Whatever those things are, I encourage you to write them down for a solid month. This will establish self-inventory as a habit. As you continue writing them down, you may find you're discovering patterns in your behavior. Areas of your personal improvement that bubble up to the top as being frequent offenders in your day. If you start seeing those frequent offenders in your behavior-your attitudes, your personality, your values alignment-that's when you can take those issues and put them into the change process. Start asking yourself about them:

- Why am I feeling this way?
- What's behind this thought?
- Why am I behaving this way?

Get to the truth of the matter, then challenge those truths, as they may be truth ceilings. You now know how to do that because we've done it for five chapters. And once you challenge them, make sure at the end you're identifying all of your choices for moving forward and make a different choice. Make a choice in alignment with your values, the type of person you want to be, and one who honors their own wants and needs.

One thing I know for sure, doing the same thing over and over again does not get a different result. If you are evaluating and taking a personal inventory every night before you go to bed and you're not making different choices, nothing is going to change.

11
EVERYBODY WINS

Talking about winning automatically brings up losing. In a way, we are conditioned to think in terms of winning and losing. When I think of winning and losing, my mind immediately takes me to the arena of sports. I am in no way a sports aficionado, but I do understand the emotional energy spent in my hometown when it is time for the Buckeyes to play...and trust me, we like to win. Communities across the globe love to root for their teams in all kinds of sporting events, whether team or individual sports. In most sports, a record is kept via rankings, points, distances and times. There are many ways we measure winning. Regardless of how we categorize a "win," we categorize, nonetheless. And in order for there to be a winner, there must be a loser or even losers.

But when it comes to leading people, I'm not so sure the same type of record-keeping is effective at engaging the hearts, minds and hands of those we lead. Maybe the concept of winning and losing is great for sports but not so great for the way we approach people and leadership.

RESISTANCE TO EVERYBODY WINS

I love introducing the idea "Everybody Wins" in workshops, especially with teams. Reactions to the term vary somewhat, but tend to polarize to one of two responses: *Yeah, duh* or *No way*. But this is not a fifty-fifty split; in fact, the most common response tends to favor the negative side. I've spent lots of time with these audiences, teams, and even in discussions with individuals to try to uncover the resistance to Everybody Wins. In those times of discovery, I found a few consistent areas of the resistance of the groups. Those who are brave enough to voice their struggle with the idea of everybody winning often have valid arguments. At least on the surface.

Everybody Gets a Trophy

The fear I hear voiced most often in relationship to Everybody Wins is that what I'm saying is everybody gets a trophy; this notion seems unfair. In fact, this particular pushback is most often associated with younger generations who grew up in time where kids on a little league team each received a trophy for showing up and participating, whether or not the team actually had a winning record. I am not here to argue this in particular, but rather to simply state, Everybody Wins does not mean "Everybody gets a trophy".

People Don't Get What They Deserve

Another fear surrounding Everybody Wins is that some may not get what they deserve. Or conversely, some may *not* get what they *do* deserve. Think about the judgment in that statement, that you as an individual get to decide what everybody deserves or doesn't deserve, including yourself. If you're like me, you have plenty of evidence in your life that you don't always get what you deserve; some of those instances were in your favor and some were not. There were times I worked very hard for a promotion and was passed up. I felt I did not get what I deserved. And, once when I was a kid, I took a candy bar from a local store on a dare and didn't get caught. I, too, did not get what I deserved.

Am I advocating for breaking the law or not standing up for yourself at work when you deserve a promotion? Of course not. But I am pointing out that each of us have lives filled with things we deserved and did not deserve. This idea that Everybody Wins should be about fairness is not realistic. What one person deserves and doesn't deserve can be dubious and extremely subjective and yes, in leadership roles we must evaluate, critique, and even judge at times. We must evaluate employees and assess the success or failure of initiatives, programs and performance. Hopefully, however, those evaluations are based on measurable standards applied equitably across the organization.

But if our expectation of everybody winning is that we all get the good stuff we deserve and none of the bad stuff we wish we didn't deserve; we're pursuing a pipe dream. Life simply does not work this way.

Everybody Gets What They Want

Another pushback I get is that Everybody Wins means everybody gets what they want. First of all, this may come from a fear that people getting what they want is inherently bad. Is it? Can people want ridiculous things at work? Sure. But for the most part, the research shows people want some pretty basic stuff, most of which is free. In fact, Gallup says employees favor job opportunities from employers who offer them "the ability to do what they do best; greater work-life balance and better personal well-being; greater stability and job security; a significant increase in income; the opportunity to work for a company with a great brand or reputation." Of particular note, "significant income" was fourth on a list of five. (Gallup 2019)

If more employers offered things to their employees like greater work-life balance, personal well-being and the ability to do what they do best...isn't the organization winning too? People getting what they want is good!

The automatic rejection of wants by a leader is dangerous for both that leader and those they lead. It's important we know how to identify our own deepest wants at work and encourage others to identify theirs. Knowing what you want on the deepest level can guide your top values which drive your decision-making and, ultimately, results. This works the same for those you lead. Let's get rid of the idea that people getting what they want is about giving into a bratty child. It simply is not true.

And let's be clear: do you always get everything that you want *all the time*? No. So, it stands to reason, not everyone else will get what they want either. But willingness to know what those wants are and allowing space for those wants to be expressed, is super important. You may find a lot of big overlaps between your wants and the wants of your team and wouldn't it be cool if all of you got more of those?

People Will Become Greedy with Their Needs

Much like identifying wants, identifying needs is crucial for individuals, teams, and organizations. While this may seem like a no-brainer, many people have admitted that listening to and meeting the needs of teams is exhausting work and feels like an endless battle for resources. So, they give up. Identifying your needs and the needs of your team helps to accomplish two very important yet overlooked things.

First, taking time to identify what your needs are in any given situation, gives you the information required to accomplish a goal. A need in this instance is the thing you don't have that is essential to reaching whatever the stated goal is. And, with any goal that involves others, they all have needs too. When was the last time you worked on a project or started a new initiative and before embarking on a solution, took time to identify what each stakeholder needed to accomplish that goal?

Most of my professional experiences involved being told what the problem was and what the solution was going to be. My job was to figure out my part in that solution and make it happen. No one asked me what I needed for my part in that solution. I would argue that solutions were chosen without evaluating the needs of the very people expected to implement the solution, costing the organization precious time and people resources, not to mention a drop-in morale and reduced discretionary effort. Why? My impression was the organization didn't care about me because they never bothered to ask what I needed to accomplish what it is they wanted done. The needs in any given situation or initiative can be as small as office supplies to as large as a company-wide learning initiative. Show me a leader who doesn't care about the needs of their team and I'll show you a leader who also doesn't pay attention to their own needs. The lack of needs identification spells unhealthy groups of people at work.

Everybody Wins is not about trophies and fairness; it's also not about giving into all the wants and needs of a team.

What is Everybody Wins?

Everybody Wins is at the core, the central nervous system of the servant leader. Everybody Wins stems from a core *belief* that the win can be found for as many people as possible if we just look for the wins. This concept or even mindset applies to things at work such as problem-solving, conflict management, change management, and even goal setting. The same application then can be made for your personal life. The servant leader approaches situations from an opportunistic perspective that sounds something like, "I wonder how we can solve this problem, creating a win for as many people involved as possible?" They start from this approach and truly believe the win for all can be found. But how do we create this new way of thinking and believing?

'EVERYBODY WINS' FOR YOU

Inspired by the work of James Rores of Floriss Group, I want to break down an adaptation of his Collecting WINS model. (Rores 2019) James created Collecting WINS as a servant leader approach to developing sales leaders and teams by viewing sales as a leadership competency. Here, I'm taking more of a personal application of his work so as to

164

create the broadest function of his model. WINS stands for: Wants, Impacts, Needs, and Solutions.

Before I dive into WINS, I ask you to think about your life as a whole: your work, family, friends, hobbies, finances, and free time. Now, dream a little. What would all those areas look like if they were *ideal*. It's okay to want more and better, especially if your impetus is to create value for yourself, your family, and those around you. Go ahead, picture your best life for all of the areas of your life.

Some people need help thinking this way. Most of us dream too small, in that we think of what seems attainable *today*. Resist the urge to think in terms of *how* you will reach this ideal destination. Instead, just think of *what* that ideal destination looks like. Take a moment to just soak in the feeling of attaining those ideal destinations in the various areas of your life. Is an ideal destination to write a book? For me it was. I began to allow myself to feel what I imagined it would feel like to have the book written. I pulled that feeling into my *now* and allowed that imagined future state to fuel me today to reach it. Part of imagining wins for yourself is feeling as if you've achieved the wins today. You can create the "winning emotions" before the win ever occurs. If that seems a little to woo-woo for you, maybe the WINS steps below will help.

WANTS Questions

In thinking about your ideal state in any area of your life, ask yourself discovery questions. As an example, I've used pursuing an ideal job as my subject:

- What do I want to be doing for work?
- How much money do I want to make?
- What kind of people do I want to work with?
- What does my office look like?
- What does my schedule look like?
- How much freedom do I have?
- Am I traveling? To where? How often?
- What do I want to be feeling when I am working?

- What makes me want to change or pursue this kind of work/work environment?

Give yourself a stretch where you feel just a little bit of discomfort with your answers, but not so much that there's no way you can believe in the possibilities. For example, if you want to be a linebacker for the Dallas Cowboys and you are fifty-eight years old and weigh a hundred and forty pounds, your "want" may be outside the realm of possibility. (But who knows? Stranger things have happened.) Knowing what you want essentially creates goals.

Your wants are your goals.

A Note About Goals

Most people have heard of SMART goals, which are traditionally written as Specific, Measurable, Achievable, Relevant, and Time-bound. (AchieveIt n.d.) But I like to use Ken Blanchard's version which is a slight variation: Specific, Motivating, Attainable, Relevant, Trackable. (Blanchard n.d.) While they seem very similar, I'm particularly drawn to "Motivating." This speaks to the idea that our goals should be both relevant to the mission and vision of an organization and motivating to the person who is achieving the goal. In essence, this model for SMART goals is an Everybody Wins move. Simply put: as you home in on your goals, I highly recommend writing them so that the words on paper are Specific and Trackable, that you are motivated by them, believe they are attainable, and are relevant to your organization.

IMPACTS Questions

When asking yourself Impacts questions, you are trying to discover the case for your goals or wants. Here are some Impacts questions to ask yourself:

- What has not worked in the past? What happened?
- Why do I want to make this change now?
- What are the positive and negative impacts of attaining what I want?

- Who is impacted by my goals? In what ways?

Looking at impacts helps us understand both the cost and the payoffs of achieving our wants. This is an important step because sometimes, we have not fully evaluated what we may have to give up achieving something. Every goal has a price. Equally as true, evaluating impacts gets us excited because we have identified the benefits of achieving our wants.

NEEDS Questions

At this point in the process, back up from your big picture and you ask yourself:

- What is between me and my wants?
- What's missing now that has prevented me from realizing my deepest wants?
- What would it take to get there?

It's important to get as clear of picture as possible about the distance between where you are and where you want to be. This distance is the gap or the *needs*.

To close the gap as much as possible, a part of this phase needs to include identifying anything happening now that is closer to the want than you realized. Or, what is within your power now to bring you closer to one of those wants. Maybe you aren't as far off from those wants as you thought. Sometimes, we don't realize the quick wins within our grasp *today*.

When I first engaged in this exercise, one of the wants I identified was my physical work environment, both the aesthetics and the locations. I knew I wanted a flexible environment where I could work from home as well as have an office outside of my home but close by. And whether at home or an office, there was a certain look in the space I wanted to feel creative and peaceful. After I gave myself this clarity, I realized there were aspects of those wants I could take action on now and other aspects I could plan for in the next phase, *Solutions*. Once you have clarity on the needs or the gaps, you can begin to focus on them for solution-finding, because without Wants, Impacts, and Needs identified, there is no problem. Remember:

Want + Impact + Need = The Problem

SOLUTIONS Questions

If you're like me, you identify a goal (want) and immediately begin to look for solutions. This is dangerous in sales but just as dangerous personally. Here's why: when you jump to solutions before identifying Impacts and Needs, you quickly begin to "count the cost" of each solution and make your Solutions decision based on commodity-thinking. This kind of thinking leads you to quick fixes and Band-Aid solutions that actually never solve your real problem and have the potential to cause more issues.

Additionally, the Want + Impact + Need discovery process ensures you ask enough thought provoking questions to create the awareness you need to actually achieve your goals.

Solutions Questions, then, are the questions and considerations you take after you've done the work of identifying wants, impacts and needs. You ask yourself what *solutions* address the *wants*, take into account the *impacts* and fulfill the stated *needs*? In other words, instead of just jumping to possible solutions, you wait to evaluate asking what solutions might work until you first look at wants, impacts and needs.

This is the process of making a commitment to winning for yourself first. Once you can get good at winning for yourself, you can start thinking about identifying wins for everyone.

EVERYBODY WINS FOR OTHERS

Think about the people you work with. Think about who your work touches and influences, for example, your co-workers, your boss, direct reports, collaborators, vendors, and customers. These individuals or groups of individuals are stakeholders. Now, think about a specific situation, like the implementation of a new initiative at work.

Socializing support for a new initiative across all of affected stakeholders is a servant leader move. This act ensures buy-in from as many people as possible and expresses care for those whom the initiative touches. When you come from a place of truly caring both about the people impacted and the initiative itself, you create a scenario where your servant leader culture is echoed by your actual behaviors. Do you see the win/win here? Do you see the wins for you, the initiative itself, and for others?

WANTS Questions

- What do you want the initiative to accomplish?
- What is the end result?
- What do you want for the people involved in the initiative-not just related to the tasks, but also related to their growth?
- What's the big picture you're trying to achieve with this initiative?
- Do you have any deal-breakers for yourself? What are they? What do you want?

IMPACTS Questions

Now that you have a clear picture of what this new initiative is going to accomplish, now think about each of those same stakeholders and figure out how that's going to impact each of them. I highly recommend you don't guess but ask those stakeholders. Bring them into this process. Remember: when we consider the impacts of our wants, we may realize some impacts are greater than we had planned and maybe aren't worth the cost.

- What does this initiative accomplish for me? For the affected stakeholders? In other words, what will achieving the wants accomplish for my boss, my direct reports, vendors, customers, our organization, and the community?
- What bad thing will happen if we don't get what we want/don't achieve our goals?

NEEDS Questions

What do each of the affected stakeholders need in order to reach the stated wants? (Don't forget to include yourself!) This is going to give you your gaps. The needs of accomplishing a new initiative vary from stakeholder to stakeholder. Additionally, there are general needs around communication and possibly internal and external marketing.

But until you know these needs and wants of both your initiative and the people that are involved in the initiative, you won't know where they overlap and how to draw the biggest win for the greatest number of people. A mistake I often see leaders make is they come up with a big idea that's really great. They have no idea what their people want and, more importantly, need in order to help them accomplish that big idea. Furthermore, they never consider the impact of this initiative. They just expect everybody to get on board. That is not Everybody Wins. Ultimately, as a leader, you are responsible for the people you hired and who work for you. If they are winning, you are winning too. You cannot win if the people working for you are losing. It simply doesn't work.

- What resources are needed to implement this initiative?
- What do we not have yet that is necessary?

SOLUTIONS Questions

With needs or gaps identified, true solutions can be considered. All too often, new initiatives are created to address needs that have already been met and because of a lack of due diligence on identifying the true wants and impacts, solutions are implemented when not needed.

When considering solutions to implementing a new initiative, it's important to ask things like:

- What has worked/not worked before? Why?
- What possible solutions actually address the wants, take into consideration the impacts, and meet actual needs?
- Of those best solutions, which one creates the greatest opportunity to benefit the most people?

This may seem like a lot of extra work but trust me, once you get used to thinking this way, the time is lessened and well spent. It's significantly better than implementing a solution that has not been properly vetted and results in failure.

Go, No-go

Let's be realistic, sometimes wins cannot be found. In my experience, this is a sign that we are not ready to move forward, and that's okay.

In personal relationships, maybe one person is not willing to reconcile if there's been a conflict. Well, guess what? If someone else is unwilling to reconcile and get on the same boat, it's really hard to row forward. That's okay. Helping other people find a win while you identify your wins as well does involve the willingness of other people. Most often, this problem is found in conflicts. Don't believe for a second that just because you're at a no-go spot that the win can never be found. Finding yourself at a no-go spot simply opens up a new set of choices and problems to solve. It's not a dead end. It just might mean it can't be found for now or in the way you originally imagined.

Your willingness in attempting to find a win with that person will go really far with them even if they don't respond today. Ultimately, you're not responsible for that outcome. As a servant leader, you're responsible to stay committed to this belief that it can be found, but you're not trying to force outcomes, especially as it pertains to the will of another human being.

A different example of a no-go situation might be in times of crisis. One time while working in a corporate setting, we were rolling out a new national product. I was part of the team planning this roll out and even doing some of the implementation. There were multiple times the timeline had to change and flux. In those changes, there were people that normally would have been brought into the change process who weren't. Unfortunately, they were simply left out for the sake of time and a lot of that lack of communication was outside my control.

Had I known then what I know now, would it change the pace at which I had to make decisions and move? Not really. But it would have changed the way I communicated those things. Our crunched timeline may have meant skipping over a department head to get a decision made more quickly, but it didn't have to mean a lack of communication about the reasons why. Today, this would have been a no-go for me. No movement until the rationale for actions taken had been expressed.

As a servant leader, a no-go for me is sacrificing relationships. If I need to rush a process due to an unforeseen circumstance, I will make sure to at least explain this fact to whoever it affects. The collateral damage of non-communication in times of crisis is almost always a loss of trust. Loss of trust in a work relationship is not worth the time saved in non-communication. The quality of my work relationships comes before the work.

In times of crisis, we don't always have time to pull everyone in a room and figure out what everyone's wants and needs are and draw that big circle and do the official Everybody Wins practice. But what we can do is over-communicate our commitment to finding a win by explaining why we had to rush a process when something went beyond our control. Even the care, caution, and concern it took to explain why we had to act and react a certain way can go a long way toward preserving relationships. And that's the key.

In times of crisis, we may have to truncate the connection process, but we don't have to sacrifice vulnerability and transparency in the name of something urgent.

EVERYBODY WINS EVERYWHERE

As you think about your own personal life, maybe at home or with your relationships, take a look at the people in your life and common issues around personal relationships. One of the common issues that affect every personal relationship is conflict. How do we find an Everybody Wins solution when there's conflict? Really, it's the same process just applied in a different context.

Wants: What do each of us want as far as a resolution? Are there overlaps? Focus on these.

Impacts: What positive and negative consequences occur if we get/don't get what we want? Are we willing to live with any identified negative impacts? Are we excited about the payoffs/benefits?

Needs: What would it take for each of us to get to the shared resolution?

Solutions: Which solution(s) create the broadest possibility for a win for all?

Why don't we actively utilize an Everybody Wins approach? The answer is simple: we want solutions fast. And in the above scenarios, we can't find a solution fast. We have to involve others, ask what they want and need, be prepared to hear things we don't like or that don't align with our vision. As a servant leader, are we willing to entertain that we may not have had the best idea?

I hope so.

Actively seeking a win for everybody actually increases the chances it will be found because people will be inspired by the commitment of such win-finding. Motivations still matter. If the motivation in a relationship, or as a leader, is to manipulate people and get what you want, ultimately, people will be able to sniff that out. If your motivation is from fear or that you're trying to prove yourself to people because you want to be seen as this super awesome person, people will sniff that out, too.

The servant leader commits to Everybody Wins because they believe it's good. The servant leader believes that when other people are winning, they are winning too. And when we are winning, the whole organization is winning. They believe that when organizations win, the entire community is lifted and benefits from those wins. Servant leaders don't engage in Everybody Wins to manipulate or because they read it in a (this) book, and it seems like a good leadership thing to do. Rather, the servant leader embarks on Everybody Wins out of a true sense of caring. There are plenty of leaders play-acting at leadership, taking on the latest leadership personality checklist to get approval from those they lead. This is nothing more than an ego-driven need to be loved and for approval.

The servant leader needs *to* love. Their primary concern is not what they want from you but what they want *for* you.

Like everyone else, you'll have specific wants and needs. Your wants and needs shouldn't be ignored. They should be acknowledged and evaluated for how they impact others in an open discussion with those affected by your wants and needs. Sometimes, what I want or need have too big of a negative impact on others. I re-evaluate them and maybe choose something else with a reduced negative impact.

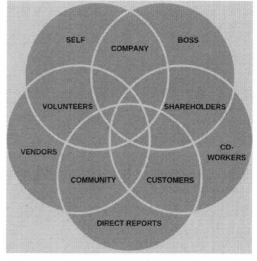

Figure 10

Imagine each of these circles (Fig. 10) represents

174

individuals and/or groups involved in any given situation. This can include anyone involved in a conflict or in promoting a new idea at work, or maybe anyone involved in goal setting. If you could put each of their names in one of those circles and then got very clear on what each of their topline needs were and some of their wants, and then try to find where all of those things overlapped, making sure not to leave yourself out of the diagram, you may find that there's a great way to draw a pretty large overlapping circle in the middle.

Please know you will never hit all the wants and needs of everyone involved. That simply isn't possible. This is about an effort towards meeting as many needs and some of the wants as possible knowing that it's not perfect. The key is that no one person's needs get met at the expense of another person's needs.

Does this sound possible? I believe Everybody Wins is possible. Your belief will drive this outcome, however. If you believe it can be found, it can be found. Your brain will move in the direction of your belief. If you don't believe it can be found, well, it cannot be found. It's that simple. This is about belief. Everybody Wins only works when the individual believes in the process and gets relentless and tenacious about finding the wins for all including self. It actually gets pretty fun. It's sort of an adventure to practice this intentionally and I encourage you to do so.

12
SERVANT LEADERSHIP IN YOUR WHOLE LIFE

Adopting a servant leader mindset can positively impact your entire life. I've often said that great leadership development is not done in a silo but rather creates growth for a person that impacts every area of their life. Servant leadership can be embraced by all and in all. If you influence anyone anywhere, you are a leader and you have various aspects to your life beyond work. While this book does take more of a professional leadership perspective in many areas, make no mistake: servant leadership is for your whole life and is for every person.

You may have picked up this book because you are a leader of people. Being in actual leadership and loving and caring about people doesn't make you a servant leader, but it's a good start. What I'm more interested in is the shifting mindset, getting honest about motivations, long-held beliefs, and resultant actions so as to begin to embody the kind of leader that we want to be in every area of our life…whether or not we have people who actually work for us.

While your journey into a servant leaders' mindset will be different from mine, I'd like to describe for you what this journey might look like for your whole life. My hope is to give more concrete imagery to applying the mindsets presented here in a way that moves from your inside (mindset, philosophy, beliefs) to outside (behaviors and habits). I do believe; however, you can take the opposite approach or even a simultaneous approach. In other words, you can start by changing habits and then challenging beliefs. Or you can challenge your beliefs while at the same time, addressing behaviors that don't align with the results you truly want. Regardless, the most powerful result was when I first worked on myself so that's where I'll start here.

SELF

So many leadership books and models focus on how the leader shows up for others first, by providing strategies and tactics for behavior. But without a mindset shift those new leader behaviors may not stick. And while new leader actions are wonderful and important, I believe beginning externally misses a huge opportunity of awareness that can impact everything else. Let's look at the five mindsets at work *in you* first.

Vulnerability

This is where you uncover the motives that are inspired by proving yourself to others or by playing small in life. These are opposite sides of the same coin. Both are hiding mechanisms because they both avoid vulnerability. To become more vulnerable, you start first by admitting those true motivations and doing the work on yourself. This is where you get really honest about where your thinking, emotions, actions, and results don't line up with the ideal servant leader and admit them...at least to yourself. Remember: you have thoughts about your life that create feelings; those feelings stimulate your actions, and your actions give you your results. I cannot stress this enough. If you aren't getting the results you want in your personal life, in your relationship, or with your friends at work, you are responsible for those results. This is good news. This means you have a role to play in changing those results. It takes a lot of personal vulnerability to get out of the victim mentality.

When we stop blaming others and take responsibility, the real work of vulnerability begins. Then we can challenge and change our own belief systems that keep us from showing up the way we really want, and that keep us from getting the results we truly desire.

Spirituality

For yourself, this might be quite a long process, and please understand none of this is linear. This is a lifelong endeavor. For yourself, spirituality is taking time to discover and connect to a higher purpose and seeing it in every area of your life. You have an inner purpose that is simply your being. It is your awareness. It is the *you that is you*. You have an outer purpose that is your doing. Your outer purpose is informed by your talents, skills and abilities. When you become aware of the impact of your inner purpose on your outer purpose you can begin to connect to a higher purpose.

Surrender

Surrender is about identifying all the ways that you spin your emotional wheels attempting to control the situations of your life, believing that by doing so you can prevent bad outcomes or create good outcomes. Surrender is putting that kind of behavior down by picking up those things that you absolutely can be in charge of, which are your own thoughts, your feelings, and your actions. Surrender is the daily reminder to self that you have no possible way of controlling what's going to happen that day and eventually accepting that fact.

Detachment

Detachment is a further letting go process that moves you beyond the emotional letting go in surrender to the mental letting go, where you detach from what used to be your old mechanisms of behavior that temporarily calmed your fears. It's the cognitive understanding that those things don't work anymore, and new behaviors must be employed. It's a commitment to not pick up what you have already laid down emotionally. Detachment allows you to evaluate your circumstances from a neutral place of nonreaction and see the world for what it is so it can be accepted. Detachment is a process of realizing people get to be who they want to be, just like you get to be who you want to be. So rather than focus on who you wish others were being to you, you might as well focus on who you want to be.

Gratitude

Here you begin actively looking for areas of your life in which to become present so that you can see what is good, what is actually perfect right now, and using those images of gratitude as guideposts, seeing what you really, truly value. Gratitude is the starting place for getting clear on what you really value so that all of the rest of your external pursuits can be honed and focused on those values. In this way, gratitude helps you say no when you need to and yes when you want to.

HOME

Extending our new mindsets to those closest to us at home will eventually be a natural progression of our growth. To me "home" represents relationships outside of the workplace. Home is where your family and friendships live.

Vulnerability

Vulnerability in our home life means we open up to those closest to us about our past motivations that might have caused harm (only when doing so does no further harm). Vulnerability at home can also mean that we stop doing it all on our own; we ask for help (out loud, not through unspoken expectations. Unspoken expectations are the opposite of vulnerability). It means we become willing to be aware when we are not being vulnerable. This kind of vulnerability opens us up to potentially greater hurt with relationships; we always must remember to be perceptive in the kind of vulnerability we give to those around us.

Spirituality

Applied to home, spirituality means that we see the value and connection between our internal environment and the environment that we are part of creating at home, in our family, and friendships. We are responsible for what is in our Hula Hoop. Everyone else is responsible for what is in theirs. But there is the space between us in relationships and we are one hundred percent responsible for our fifty percent of those relationships. We understand our spiritual life impacts the 'space between' one another's Hula Hoop. Again, if we don't like the results that we have in the environment of home, we commit to two things: admitting through vulnerability what our part was in creating the lack of optimal results and being aware of the thoughts, feelings, and actions that were our part in the situation.

The more aware we are of how we show up to others in our home, the less those old behaviors occur. Awareness and presence help reduce old habits. In these actions, we take on a cooperative role with our home environment on a spiritual level, seeing that all things are connected. And we have a responsibility to look at our place in the home environment.

Surrender

Surrender in the home is one of the most difficult processes because it's an emotional letting go of controlling others in the family and friend groups. Very few actually set out to control others, but with this new awareness around surrender, we find that sometimes the hardest thing to surrender is the emotional responses we have to the behaviors and choices of others closest to us.

Being able to have interactions at home with others, void of negative emotional internal reactions, allows us to enjoy those relationships more. Many times, we don't enjoy the relationships that we have with loved ones like parents, in-laws, and even our children, because we're unhappy with their behavior. We've become emotionally tied to their behavior to the point that it drives us to dissatisfaction and unhappiness. We falsely believe if the people closest to us would just act a certain way, we wouldn't feel the way we feel about them. This is not true. Surrender here is the willingness to put those emotional reactions down.

Detachment

Detachment then is the cognitive recognition-the thought patterns-that allow us to walk away from behavior we don't like (physically or just mentally). Sometimes the behaviors around us are truly damaging, like abusive relationships. Yes, we should physically detach from that environment. Aside from those obvious circumstances, all of us can stand to mentally detach and the best way we know how to do that is with these thoughts: My friends and my family are allowed to be who they are. They are allowed to do what they want, just like I am. And, furthermore, that is to be celebrated. This live-and-let-live mentality is a thought process that we go through that allows us to move beyond tolerating those around us to celebrating them.

Gratitude

When we bring gratitude into our home, we intentionally become aware of the gifts that are gained by letting people be who they are. We see the tension we previously created by wanting people to be different and instead choose to be *grateful for who they actually are*. We have new tools to let go of that tension. We thereby open up new levels of appreciation for others in our life. Now that we have separated ourselves emotionally and mentally from others in a healthy way, we can see them for who they are and actually see the gifts that they bring to our life, rather than being stuck in the emotional rat wheel we previously created in our minds.

WORK

I began practicing these mindsets at work first, and then gradually saw the same issues show up in my personal life.

You may start with self and finally apply to work. It doesn't matter the approach, but if you have a lot of pain at work, may I suggest you at least try them out there first? You'll give yourself a lot of relief in a place where you spend the majority of your time, improving your overall quality of life as a result.

Vulnerability

At work, vulnerability definitely has a place. Vulnerability may simply start as an, "I don't know." For many leaders, not knowing the answer means bad leadership. This is a limiting belief. No one human being has all the answers in every situation, nor can they anticipate every need in order to learn the answer in advance. Such a silly expectation we place on ourselves.

From there, being vulnerable at work means becoming willing to admit when we are wrong and when we needed help. Even more powerful, vulnerability is inviting others into our thought process and being open to allow others with less power to influence decisions, our thinking, and even a specific direction. Finally, vulnerability is the willingness to be known by those around us at work.

Spirituality

Spirituality at work may seem strange. Remember, this is an internal thing for us. Applying spirituality to work then, is about helping others connect to a higher purpose. Creatively painting a picture of a higher purpose for your team is a spiritual practice, because you invite others into the exploration of that which is bigger than us all. This act comes from a place of caring that those team members see a connection between what they do and something-anything-higher than themselves, even if that higher purpose has nothing to do with the organization.

We don't need to do draw every single individual task to the mission of the organization necessarily. We do actively look for opportunities to help those around us find a higher purpose in their everyday work because we know this is a win for them. Sometimes this is providing a "why" along with the "what" when we delegate. Even that small act will tap into increased engagement, discretionary effort, and create, more importantly, a lot more fulfillment for employees.

Surrender

Surrender can be a challenging balance between holding people accountable without utilizing old controlling behaviors of emotional manipulation, believing that "if we do this, our employees will do that." We now focus on what we can control. What are those things? We can control our efforts to equip those around us, who work for us. When we embark on new projects and delegate responsibility, we over-communicate the who, what, when, where, why, and how ("how" to a point-we want those who work for us to have a say), and then emotionally let go of the results and the outcomes. This means the people who work for us, whom we have adequately equipped, are alone responsible for their own results, and we have surrendered the fears around that process.

Detachment

Detachment at work can take the form of letting go of drama so as to remain more objective. It's a suspension of judgement for the purpose of remaining in a calm nonreactive state. In this state, we can better serve others, extend empathy when needed and see our many choices as leaders when drama arises.

Gratitude

Gratitude at work is when we actively look for things to appreciate and be thankful for at work and expresses them regularly. This dynamic seeking takes the form of scheduled time. For example, we set aside time every Friday to write thank-you notes, expressing specifically what each person did that made us take notice, how what they did helped us, and why it is connected to the higher purpose of the organization. This takes more time, yes, but the results are good for us and others on a physiological level. We begin making a daily practice of thinking both personally and professionally of the things that went well every day, and how grateful we are for them. This creates a positive virtuous cycle of gratitude throughout the organization.

COMMUNITY

I almost left out a section on community because some of it seemed too simple. However, I believe for some people, utilizing these mindsets in a broader way might be helpful, especially if you struggle in any of these specific areas in the bigger community in which you live.

Vulnerability

Vulnerability in the community is a willingness for us to become proximate to problems in our cities. This brings up fears around people groups with whom we are less familiar. Vulnerability then is getting honest about those fears around community service and helping those at risk, talking to people who know more than we do, and educating ourselves. Let's be willing to admit and face those fears.

Spirituality

The mindset of spirituality in a community is really the understanding that even the smallest act is tied to a much bigger picture-a bigger picture that is so big in fact, we cannot see all of it, we only see a part. We begin to operate from the belief that what each of us does matters to all of us. What we do in and for our community is connected to everyone and everything else. When we all do our part, no matter how small, we are all elevated.

Surrender

As we let go of our fears around serving others, we might become overwhelmed by the needs. Surrender in this instance meant letting go of the feeling that we need to help everyone, all the time, or we aren't doing enough. Surrender means focusing on what we can do just for today. We must surrender the overwhelming needs in our community and not allow the overwhelm to derail us from action. Surrender is an emotional letting go of what we simply cannot do while taking action on what we can.

Detachment

Detachment helps us accept a healthy mental outlook regarding personal homework and community action. When we look at all of our lives in realistic terms, we see that life is an ebb and flow, not really a balance at all. From a decision-making perspective, we must prioritize what we're able to do and contribute to our community as a whole. We can take a step outside the emotional components of community need and make decisions from a mental space that is supportive of what we value, our goals, the culture we're trying to create around us, and the community we want to be a part of. Detachment gives us the mental space to do this so we're not aimlessly reacting to all the overwhelming needs of our community. Detachment gives us the clarity to respond concisely, efficiently, compassionately and intelligently towards community problems.

Gratitude

We begin seeing beauty everywhere and, in every person, maybe even in every interaction. We may need to take a little break just to breathe and slow down. Sometimes, once we begin feeling gratitude at this level on a regular basis, the creative inspiration that comes can feel a tad overwhelming, but this is okay. The world really is a miraculous place when we stop and think about the visual splendor of it all.

TOO MUCH?

Do you think all of this is impossible or even Pollyanna-ish? I'm here to tell you that it's not. These descriptions are my very own journey into servant leadership. They described my journey into discovering these five mindsets. Now, you may have picked up this book to learn about a servant leader mindset, and I hope that you've grasped on to at least one new concept to challenge yourself. If embraced, you will find a new way of showing up in life-in all of your life-a way that brings a fulfillment that you may have sought for years but have been unable to find.

Yes, I want you to show up differently at work and for those around you at home. Yes, I want you to find more fulfillment and experience less frustration. Yes, I want you to find the Everybody Wins for as many people as often as possible at work.

But what I want for you most of all is to see that servant leader mindsets have a whole-life application, which means they can impact the results of your entire life. As you move forward, I encourage you to take tiny baby steps towards implementing these mindsets. When learning something new, the tendency is to think of multiple ways to apply the new knowledge. This is especially true with personal development. Rather than thinking of all the places in your life that would benefit from these mindsets, I encourage you to think of three areas of your life that cause you the most frustration.

Pause and think about that right now.

If you're unsure what the top three areas are, what's on your mind most of the time? What is taking up a lot of your emotional energy? Is it the relationship with your mother? Your spouse? Is it a contentious conversation that you had with your boss that's now turned into a standoff of silence that has lasted for months? Do you find yourself at a standstill in your community where you feel that you're inactive, unsure of where to make a difference? Whatever your top three frustrations are, just identify them. State them in a sentence or two. Write them down. Say what it is. Keep it short; state it as a problem.

Once you have three frustrations written down, pick the one that bothers you the most, the top frustration in your whole life. Look at the frustration and really critically evaluate it.

Vulnerability: Look at the frustration through the eyes of vulnerability.

Ask yourself if there are places in that situation where you're trying to hide from the truth. Are you not admitting weaknesses or that you don't know something, trying to be the hero?

Are you posturing in any way? Where are you failing to be vulnerable, humble, and open?

Spirituality: Do you see the bigger purpose here? Is there a higher meaning? What is it attached to? Or maybe you're attaching it to a bigger idea that's all made up in your mind, a bigger meaning that is negative? Is there thinking that needs to be challenged around this? The spiritual component of servant leadership is a commitment to challenging our very own mindsets on a spiritual level so as to be more aware of how our inner and outer purpose work together. Is there somewhere in this situation that maybe you're attaching to a much bigger purpose then is reasonable? Or are you not seeing this tied to a much bigger purpose at all?

Surrender: Are you emotionally connected to results? Where do you believe that your actions change the actions or emotions or thoughts of others? Where are you involved in emotionally controlling other people, places or things? Can you let that go?

Detachment: Look at your thinking and really evaluate how your thinking impacts your emotions. Are you overly attached? Where can you detach mentally from what's going on? What's the better mental story that creates the emotions you want to feel? What's the better story that keeps you in a calm, nonreactive state?

Gratitude: Is there anywhere in this situation you have failed to identify and/or express appreciation and gratitude, either for yourself, for something you're learning, or for another person?

TAKE THE CHALLENGE

I encourage you to take your situation through the servant leader mindset process (Identify, Challenge, Change). As you begin doing this, you can slowly make new choices around how you want to show up. Once you get all the truth of the matter out by weighing against these mindsets, you can challenge the areas for truth and extremes; evaluate your responsibilities and choices. You can then look at those choices and make a new choice and take action, and then eventually bring about change. As you do this, practice just the one situation every time it comes up, every time a similar thought occurs. Identify it, challenge it, and change it.

Change is possible for you. These mindsets are available to you and when embraced, even just in the beginning, you will find they bring greater degrees of joy, contentment and satisfaction to work and your whole life. My hope is that you too look back on your own development with gratitude of this knowledge, knowing you have all the power you need to change your own life; a power that has been there all along.

Bibliography

AchieveIt. n.d. *The History and Evolution of SMART Goals.* Accessed November 12, 2019. https://www.achieveit.com/resources/blog/the-history-and-evolution-of-smart-goals.

Barbara Markway, Ph.D. and Greg Markway, Ph.D. 2019. *Brené Brown's Netflix Special Busts Six Vulnerability Myths.* May 13. Accessed November 6, 2019. https://www.psychologytoday.com/us/blog/shyness-is-nice/201905/bren-browns-netflix-special-busts-six-vulnerability-myths.

Blanchard, Ken. n.d. *A New Twist on SMART Goals.* Accessed November 12, 2019. https://www.bkconnection.com/bkblog/ken-blanchard/a-new-twist-on-smart-goals.

Brené Brown Ph.D., LMSW. 2017. *Rising Strong.* New York: Random House.

Brené Brown, Ph.D., LMSW. 2012. *Daring Greatly.* New York: Avery.

Burns, David. 1992. *Feeling Good: The New Mood Therapy.* Avon Books.

Chowdhury, Madhuleena Roy. 2019. *PositivePsychology.com.* September 4. Accessed October 20, 2019. https://positivepsychology.com/neuroscience-of-gratitude/.

Energy Leadership. 2019. *The Energy Leadership Index Assessment.* Accessed October 24, 2019. https://www.energyleadership.com/assessment.

Gallup. 2018. *News.* August 26. Accessed October 24, 2019. https://news.gallup.com/poll/241649/employee-engagement-rise.aspx.

—. 2019. *What Star Employees Want.* Accessed November 12, 2019. https://www.gallup.com/workplace/231767/star-employees.aspx.

Heath, Dan Heath and Chip. 2017. *The Power of Moments: Why Certain Experiences Have Extraordinary Impact.* New York: Simon and Schuster.

Kennon M. Sheldon, Todd B. Kashdan, Michael F. Steger. 2011. "The Future of Emotions Research Within Positive Psychology." In *Designing Positive Psychology*, by Robert A. Emmons and Anjali Mishra, 122. New York: Oxford University Press.

Lexico. 2019. *Lexico.* Accessed November 6, 2019. https://www.lexico.com/en/definition/vulnerability.

Pope, Msgr. Charles. 2018. *The Probability of You Existing at All Is Unbelievably Low.* August 28. Accessed February 22, 2020. http://blog.adw.org/2018/08/probability-existing-unbelievably-low-yet-lets-look-numbers/.

Robert F. Russell, A. Gregory Stone. 2002. March 23. Accessed September 15, 2019. http://strandtheory.org/images/Russell_Stone_-_SL_Attributes.pdf.

Robert F. Russell, A. Gregory Stone. 2002. "A review of servant leadership attributes: developing a practical model." *Leadership & Organization Development Journal* 145-157.

Robert K. Greenleaf Center for Servant Leadership. n.d. *What Is Servant Leadership.* Accessed November 4, 2019. https://www.greenleaf.org/what-is-servant-leadership/.

Rores, James. 2019. *FlorissGroup.com.* Accessed May 5, 2019. https://florissgroup.com/collecting-wins/.

Seltzer, Leon F. 2016. *Psychology Today.* June 15. Accessed December 5,

2019. https://www.psychologytoday.com/us/blog/evolution-the-self/201606/you-only-get-more-what-you-resist-why.

Sisodia, Raj. 2014. *Second Edition Firms of Endearment.* Accessed October 24, 2019. https://www.firmsofendearment.com/.

Springle, Pat. 1994. *Trusting.* Ann Arbor: Servant Publications.

The Ken Blanchard Companies. 2017. "Why a Situational Approach to Leadership Matters." *KenBlanchard.com.* Accessed November 5, 2019. https://resources.kenblanchard.com/situational-leadership-ii/why-a-situational-approach-to-leadership-matters.

The Life Coach School. 2019. "The Life Coach School." *Belief Ceilings.* July 25.

ABOUT THE AUTHOR

Shannon Lee is a former educator and sales leader turned author, facilitator, nonprofit leader and coach. Her work includes the creation of the CARE model for leadership, associated workshops and the Servant Leader Mindset coaching program. Shannon resides in Columbus, OH, where she serves as the Executive Director for Relā, a nonprofit committed to serving the learning and development needs of both the business and nonprofit community. Together with her husband, she has three amazing adult children and two Shih Tzus.

For speaking and other inquiries, you can reach Shannon directly at shannon@shannonmlee.com.

Made in the USA
Columbia, SC
21 July 2020